Cathy goes to Canberra

Cathy goes to Canberra

Doing politics differently

Cathy McGowan

Cathy goes to Canberra: Doing politics differently
© Copyright 2020 Cathy McGowan
All rights reserved. Apart from any uses permitted by Australia's Copyright Act 1968, no part of this book may be reproduced by any process without prior written permission from the copyright owners. Inquiries should be directed to the publisher.

Monash University Publishing
Matheson Library Annexe
40 Exhibition Walk
Monash University
Clayton, Victoria 3800, Australia
www.publishing.monash.edu

Monash University Publishing brings to the world publications which advance the best traditions of humane and enlightened thought.

ISBN: 9781925835908 (paperback)
ISBN: 9781925835915 (pdf)
ISBN: 9781925835922 (epub)

www.publishing.monash.edu/books/cgc-9781925835908.html

Front cover image: *Cathy McGowan on her motorbike*, 1973. Paul McGowan. From the McGowan family collection. Reproduced courtesy of Cathy McGowan.

Back cover image: *Cathy McGowan valedictory supporters*, 4 April 2019, Marco Catalano. Reproduced by permission of the Australian Broadcasting Corporation – Library Sales. Marco Catalano © 2019 ABC

Cover design: Christabella Designs

Internal design: Les Thomas

A catalogue record for this book is available from the National Library of Australia.

CONTENTS

Chapter 1   Making history 1

Chapter 2   Coming home 9

Chapter 3   A woman in agriculture 19

Chapter 4   A phone call 29

Chapter 5   Someone has to do it 43

Chapter 6   The candidate 57

Chapter 7   The campaign 67

Chapter 8   Indi turns orange 77

Chapter 9   Using the courage muscle 85

Chapter 10   Tending the patch 103

Chapter 11   Make some noise 115

Chapter 12   Is this the best our politics can be? 131

Chapter 13   A survival guide 149

Chapter 14   You can do it 163

Acknowledgments 177

About the author 181

*Dedicated to Marie and Paul McGowan
who encouraged me to
Bloom where I was Planted.*

Chapter 1

MAKING HISTORY

Election night in a hall in Wangaratta, with orange everywhere. Orange balloons. Orange streamers. Orange shirts. Orange was our colour. Orange has boldness, a little bit of optimism, some hope. It wants to be noticed. Demands it, really. Its brightness captured our movement: the intensity of our belief, our energy. Hundreds of Voices for Indi campaign volunteers buzzed around the room. Would we win? Our seat of Indi, one of a dwindling number of electorates that dated back to the beginning of Federation in 1901, had been such a reliable electorate for the Liberal and National parties and their forebears for so much of its history. I didn't think we could do it and I wasn't the only one in the room who thought that way – not by a long shot. There was a lot of tension in that hall because we'd been staffing the booths during the day and the portents hadn't been good. It just seemed to many of us that too many voters had gone out of their way to take the blue Liberal how-to-vote cards as they headed into the polling places.

In our seat, we'd worked out that of the 112,000 or so people eligible to vote, there were about 30,000 in the middle – voters willing to consider what we were advocating – who we'd need to get behind us. We estimated that up to one person in every four might be open to consider an alternative. They were our path to victory. We couldn't have them relying on old habits and putting a '1' next to the Liberal candidate on the ballot paper. But that's where we were: the counting of the votes had started as soon as the booths closed at 6pm, and I wasn't feeling good about it.

I'm simply not a Political person, not in the way most people understand it, anyway. I've never been a my-party-right-or-wrong type. I regard those people as Political with a capital 'P'. I'm lower case 'p'. I've never belonged to a party. I've never seen politics as a form of combat or sport, where my side goes into battle against someone else's side. I just don't see politics that way. The usual gumph of day-to-day party Politics has never meant much to me: the gossip and the jostling and intrigue, the minutiae that renders it more like a soap opera than anything else.

But by golly I wanted us to win. We needed to prove that what we'd been campaigning for – a different way of doing politics – could genuinely take hold in our part of the world in Victoria's northeast. A victory tonight would be nothing short of magnificent: a truly great achievement. Ever since the community group Voice for Indi had formed in 2012, inspired by the idea of converting Indi from a safe Liberal seat to a competitive, marginal electorate, I had steered well clear of investing my ego in our campaigning. But I realised in the buzzing, highly charged atmosphere of the hall that the outcome of this count was profoundly important to me.

And I wasn't even the candidate.

My parliamentary career was already behind me. I'd given my final speech in the House of Representatives five weeks earlier, after serving two terms as the member for Indi. I was gone and I was certainly happy about that. But this night, Saturday 18 May 2019, was the moment when we would find out whether my two previous election wins as an independent had been a flash in the pan. That had been the pattern since the first federal parliament. There had been many

MAKING HISTORY

independent Members of Parliament through the years but once they surrendered their seats, they were replaced by candidates from political parties. What we were aiming for in 2019 was a first: a handover from one independent to another. Voices for Indi – we changed the name, adding the 's' in 2014, and that is what I'll call it throughout this book – is not a political party, and this time our candidate was Helen Haines, who, like me, had deep and extensive ties throughout our region. Helen and her husband Phil had been involved with Voices for Indi since its early days.

As the early vote tallies trickled in, I went through mental exercises to prepare myself for disappointment. I told myself that this was alright, that we'd done what we'd set out to do: we'd won the seat twice. I got somewhere close to reconciling myself to that. But I couldn't get all the way. Here was the opportunity to make history and more importantly to prove that community engagement could prevail. The hall was set up as a mini tally-room, with a big screen registering the numbers in all of Indi's polling booths as they arrived.

Scrutineers texted in the results from each polling place and, to make it a bit more of a show, we had a small group of people on the stage putting up the numbers and trying to keep the crowd involved. As each text came through, one of them would call out the location of the polling place and ask if anyone in the crowd came from that town. If there was someone there from, say, Porepunkah, they'd come up to the stage to call out the numbers.

Fortunately, we had a bit of a buffer from the 2016 result – a little over 5 per cent. By 8.30pm Helen was still in it. But we could see that there was an unexpected swing nationally to the Morrison government. That is, a move to the Liberals and the Nationals, who were both running candidates against Helen – so they could maximise the overall

Coalition vote in our seat. Would we be able to stand up to that and the swing? The Liberals and the Nationals had put enormous resources into trying to win back Indi; the Liberals especially still regarded it as theirs by right and Voices for Indi as interlopers who'd interrupted the natural order of things. Then came a result from one of the polling places in Mansfield, historically deep blue, a reliably Liberal-voting town, although we'd managed to win it in 2016. If we could put on a decent showing there, we'd probably go on to win. Someone from Mansfield called out the result: Helen had held on. The crowd erupted.

I was in a corner of the hall with Helen's husband Phil and her son Nick. This was the moment. We caught each other's eye. We sensed – no, we knew – that if we'd avoided a wipe-out in Mansfield, we'd actually got across the line. The final count showed that Helen had won Indi by 2,816 votes. A win is always good but let me tell you that when you know you've won on the night, without having to go through days or even weeks of nail-biting counts and recounts, it's better than good – it's great. The Voices for Indi movement had succeeded in a meaningful and historic way. To borrow from Paul Keating, this was the sweetest victory of all. Not only had we engaged in politics in a way that we wanted, but we'd staved off yet another fierce campaign in the electorate by the Liberal Party. The people in our community had made a decision that they didn't want to hand back their power to a political party. They wanted something bigger and better: to be directly involved in how their local member would represent them in the federal parliament. They had chosen a way of doing politics that was in a very real sense a democratic way of doing politics. This was a deeply satisfying place to be. We had set out on a relay race and we hadn't fumbled the baton change. And tonight it was our ethos of the job of an MP – to truly represent a community – that was being passed from one runner to the next.

When Voices for Indi was formed, we wanted to foster a sustainable community movement that could show that genuine democracy could work. We didn't know whether it could work. But it had. Three election wins in a row – the first in 2013 in which we wrested the seat from the incumbent Liberal member, the second in 2016 building up our margin to more than 5 per cent against that same Liberal candidate, and then the third in 2019 in which it was secured decisively by another independent – suggests that pretty strongly, don't you think? Watching the celebrations, here's what I thought: our large, isolated community in northeastern Victoria, which isn't poverty-stricken but isn't wealthy or highly educated, which in the emerging digital age had struggled with poor telecommunications, and felt it had been taken for granted, could see a better way forward. And with the leadership that the community had provided for itself, I felt so much optimism for our community. If it could do this … what else could we do? What would it mean for other communities? For our democratic system now and in the future?

Communities can do things; rural communities can take control and can act in their own best interests. More than anything, that's what we proved. The need was there, the people were there, we were motivated and there was a huge willingness to make it work. The goodwill involved was enormous and got us through so many tense and conflictive times. Across the electorate close to 1,800 volunteers had stepped up, had gone out and talked to their neighbours. And they'd done it with such professionalism, optimism and humility, which was so important to our volunteer movement.

I've started this story in an unorthodox way, with the ending at the beginning, but that's not uncharacteristic of my approach to politics and life. It's one of my sayings: 'Begin with the end in mind.' And that way of doing things was central to what we did in Indi. After all, how else do you break the 74-year hold one side of politics has on a seat other than by doing something completely different from what has been tried before? There was simply a mountain of evidence that the old ways had stopped working.

I've just lauded our election successes, but in truth a key feature of my involvement in politics is that it has regularly played out in ways that surprised even me. This is not meant as some sort of humble brag – an attempt to make out that, gee whiz, I don't know how I found myself in federal parliament, ultimately sharing the balance of power when the Turnbull and Morrison governments lost their majority in the House of Representatives and I had prime ministers asking me if there was anything they could do for me as a way of keeping me onside. It's not that. Nor can I say that I was confident for a fair bit of the time that what I was doing as a campaigner and a local member would work out. Day after day, week after week, month after month, I was learning.

Now that it's in the past, I better understand how I came to be an MP – and how I managed to be re-elected – and that's the story I will tell you, or at least a part of it. In short, it happened because hard work and caring for the community have been central to my life for as long as I can remember, except for a confusing first year at university which, to my undying embarrassment, I failed. I'm glad I got that confession out of the way.

But without giving too much of the game away too early, I invite you to reflect on that 2019 election result in Indi. How do you think Helen won it? It's widely recognised that, in just about every electorate, the membership of the established political parties is thin. The numbers are not shared publicly, but, generally, active grassroots members are few and far between, perhaps in the scores or in the low hundreds. More often than not, the parties' head offices removed from communities will run local campaigns and deploy resources provided by big donors. Slogans and unified messaging, polls, high-concept advertising which is often quite personalised and negative, are standard-issue.

It's just about all run top-down. The big parties in one form or another have been around since Federation. They are sturdy institutions, anchored by traditions and powerful name recognition, like the best-known soft drink or cereal brands. Compare that with Voices for Indi. In our 2019 election campaign, 1,800 people formally signed up as volunteers just in our one seat. That's an incredible number in a disparate electorate where slightly less than 101,000 effective votes were cast. Compared with our political opponents, we had the people – the young, the old, on the farms, in the streets of our towns, and on the mountains from Corryong to Jamison and all places in between. At each of the three elections in which Voices for Indi has been involved, the number of campaign volunteers increased. That is the power of community: when politics relates to the local community, the community responds and the power of that community is unleashed.

That's what this book, this story, is about: what a politically active community can do. In northeast Victoria we call it the Indi way.

Chapter 2

COMING HOME

I live by myself in a farmhouse atop a hill that marks the southern end of a valley. But I am never alone. From my home, I can look across the valley to the place that made me – a dairy farm where I was raised with my late parents, Paul and Marie, and my 12 siblings. Yes, we are a big family in the Irish Catholic country tradition. My mother was one of 10 children. My father was one of six. Each morning as I look out into the Indigo Valley, 20 kilometres south of Wodonga on the Victoria–New South Wales border, I can see properties where members of my family live. I see the place next door to my childhood home where my father's brother and his wife lived and raised six of my cousins. And I see where my father's parents lived in their later years. I see the story of my life. I see the forces that made me. I see and I feel my community. I know that I belong here. I feel the history of white settlement that led me to live here and to stay here. I'm a farmer too, among other things, and have been for 40 years. I raise sheep. I grow my own vegetables.

Farming in this part of Victoria is very much part of a long family tradition. Five generations ago, in the middle decades of the 19th century, my ancestors left Ireland and England in harsh times to make a better life for themselves and their children's children's children. On my mother's side, Elizabeth Ann Brown arrived from County Cork, Ireland, in 1860. She was 20 and alone. She died at the grand age of

87 and is buried in the Tallangatta cemetery, her occupation, proudly, 'farmer'. Arriving in the Chiltern goldfields of northeast Victoria, she met and married a miner from Cornwall, John Terrill. In 1875 they selected land in the Mitta Valley just below the township of Tallangatta. Barely a year later, John Terrill was killed in a mining accident at El Dorado, leaving Elizabeth Ann to raise six children and two nephews. Our family story is replete with stories of clearing the land, dealing with floods, fires and drought, and the desperate struggle to meet the conditions to purchase that land. In 1890, 30 years after her arrival in Australia, Elizabeth Ann made the final payment on the land and won free title – an incredible achievement.

Elizabeth Ann's fourth child, Albert, was my great-grandfather. She was a woman in agriculture well before that term was even thought of and I have regarded her tenacity as an example to follow. On the other side of my family, my great-grandfather Alex Chapman worked in the post office at Wodonga. His job was to travel overnight on the train, sorting the mail so it would arrive in Melbourne ready to be delivered by 10am. My grandmother, Rose Roberta Chapman, was born in Wodonga in November 1888. She married Gladstone Robert McGowan, son of Tasmanian pub owners, in 1920 and went on to become a teacher, a mother of six children and a grand matriarch. Grannie's legacy to me was: be a teacher, know history and tell stories, have a deep sense of social justice and community service, and a lasting valuable lesson was never forget to laugh.

My father Paul was raised in middle-class Melbourne and had a love for rural Australia and interest in farming. Born in 1923, he studied agricultural science at the University of Melbourne. My mother Marie Terrill was four years younger than my father and grew up in a farming family in Rutherglen. They met when my mother was at

Tay Creggan, a local version of a finishing school run by the Ladies of the Holy Grail in the Melbourne suburb of Hawthorn. And their romance blossomed a few years later, after my father graduated and was sent by the Department of Agriculture, fortuitously, to work at the Rutherglen Research Station, next door to my mother's family farm. Marriage followed and as they started their family they settled at the dairy farm where I grew up.

When my father talked about his life, he would nominate war as the defining factor. His father had fought in World War 1, had witnessed the destruction in France and concluded that the only thing you could take with you when there was nothing left was what you had in yourself – in other words, your qualifications, your education, your attitude. Before returning to Australia from England in the wake of the war, my grandfather made good on his observation and secured qualifications as a surveyor, which became his line of work back in Melbourne. This focus on education has informed the McGowan family ever since. My father and his siblings were given a great formal education and my parents helped ensure that all 13 of their children took at least one university degree.

The Cold War that followed World War 2 was something that preoccupied my father, as it did so many Australians. My father got involved in the social organisations that in the 1950s led to the formation of the Democratic Labor Party, including the National Catholic Rural Movement, which promoted a vision of living the rural lifestyle and creating community in the country. This commitment to building community through action and participation later led him to become an active member of the Liberal Party, the Victorian Farmers Federation, a councillor for the local Shire of Chiltern and to establish a farm management consultancy business.

Pretty clearly, my family environment was extensive and all-encompassing. My paternal and maternal grandparents living nearby had a huge impact on me. They lived and breathed how you should live a good life. My McGowan grandmother, especially, adhered strongly to her personal principles of decency; she was almost Victorian in her values. Along with my uncle and family living next door, there was a real community spirit. We knew we belonged. Family was important. Leadership and community involvement through local government and social organisations was expected. We pursued a goal of leaving the world a better place.

With an ever-expanding bunch of children and extended family growing up, there were disagreements and squabbling from time to time, but no aggression. My early memories are of a pretty idyllic arrangement. We would work on the farm with our dad on the weekends and that was exciting, a pleasure and a joy. We all had chores and jobs to do and we mostly loved doing them. As well as running the home and family, mum managed an extensive vegetable garden, chooks and an orchard, and in her spare time was a spinner and weaver, hobbies she passed on to me.

But I was exposed to some of the ways the outside world worked when I started taking the bus to the Catholic primary school in Beechworth, about 20 kilometres from home. The bus took the kids in our area to the Beechworth schools – state schools and Catholic. The shock of being bullied by the older state school kids just because we were Catholic stays with me to this day. Of course, this was in the late 1950s, a more sectarian time than now. Let's face it: people like my father's friends in the National Catholic Rural Movement had helped to form their own essentially Catholic political party in the form of the DLP.

But there were also class divisions at play too. Because we were dairy farmers' kids, and Catholics to boot, the state school kids looked down on us. The reason it made such an impact on my memory is because it was my first understanding of discrimination in a class context. The animosity towards the Catholics on the bus was directed at all of us – we numbered probably around 20. I knew it wasn't just about me; it had everything to do with the fact that we were not them, we were the 'other'. We were Catholics and we were dairy farmers' kids.

The other thing that shocked me was that the implied threat of violence in the bullying – sometimes it actually involved acts of violence – was so foreign to the environment of the community that I'd been used to. The older girls from the Catholic families would look after us younger ones when we were singled out, but in those early years the bus trips were tense. I can't say the experience was searing in terms of personal psychology, but it imprinted in my mind that this was how the world works, that some people would gang up on other people, bullies existed and you needed to have a strategy to deal with it.

An important lesson from those years was to have a strategy: my parents made this quite plain to me and my sisters. When we arrived home after school and complained about the bullying, we weren't allowed to whinge about how it was unfair. There was no cosseting. What they did was to tell us that we had to use our wits to sort it out. They didn't abandon us to it; they'd suggest strategies. From my father came theories about how the real world worked and from my mother came pragmatic advice on how to stop the taunts from escalating. As my father had grown up in Melbourne, he hadn't experienced that level of discrimination, whereas my mother was from the country and had a deeper understanding of how to manage the politics of the school bus. I can see all these years later that I was getting some good training for being a crossbench MP both at home and on the school bus. I had to learn how to navigate my way through conflict and reach accommodations. Anybody who's grown up in a big family or small rural community will tell you how much of your time is spent on negotiating and building a support base so you don't fight alone.

Seventeen years separated the oldest and the youngest of the 13 children in our house. I was part of the first group. I was number four, greeting the world in 1953. We formed the 'old' group of siblings in the family because a few years passed before the next group of siblings arrived. In fact, depending on how you look at it, there were three mini-families based on when the children were born. As the youngest in the first group, I was constantly trying to keep up with my older sisters. I felt that sense of competition, a need to prove myself, and I was learning how to do whatever they did. Clearly, I wasn't as old or as clever as them, so I had to learn how to manage up. I also had to learn about alliances in the family, getting the little kids on side. It was exactly like that for my other siblings, too. Growing up in that farmhouse was a degree course in leadership and conflict resolution and alliances in the politics of a big family. It was so deeply ingrained in me and my approach to life and work, I've often found myself bewildered that other people haven't developed these skills when, of course, very few of us have that sort of upbringing.

Although there was competition and the predictable amount of friction that you'll get when people are around each other in numbers for long times, it was a pretty harmonious home. Our parents ran a regimented household – the older kids were assigned a sort of mentor/protector role for individual younger siblings, for example – and the regimentation was usually directed towards efficiency and effectiveness, and had the side-effect of developing problem-solving and conflict resolution and the ability to ride through life's ups and downs in each of us. Learning how to listen and build a support base did come in handy when I found myself a community candidate running for federal parliament many years later.

If not for the passion for education that characterised my family, there's probably little chance that I'd be telling this story about becoming a federal MP. There's a good chance I'd be a farmer, enjoying my life in Indigo Valley. Yet my parents' expectations were high and they wanted all of us to reach our potential, and no matter how average any of us was as a student, we would each go on to at least attain a bachelor's degree. So I grew up knowing that I had to work hard to get to uni. I'm not one of the brightest buttons in our family; some of my siblings won scholarships when they matriculated, but not me. My marks weren't good enough to secure a scholarship. I'd wanted to study law at the University of Melbourne but had no way of paying for it, so I accepted a Victorian Government studentship to cover my tuition fees. In the early 1970s a studentship was basically an enlightened form of indentured labour: the Victorian Department of Education paid your fees and in return you were required to complete your degree and a one-year teaching qualification and then teach within the state school system for several years.

At the department's urging, I enrolled in an Arts degree at Monash University, majoring in history and economics. But, as I've already mentioned, I failed first year, having spent too much time in the cafeteria in the student union building and discovering boys and motor bikes. In the family, this academic stumble was unexpected and unprecedented but I was fully accepting of it. I determined that I'd just come home and work on the farm, but my parents weren't having a bar of that. They told me that not only would I have to return to Monash and repeat the year but that I'd have to get a job and pay my own way. As I spent the following year making up for the subjects that I'd failed, I worked at the Peters ice cream factory near Monash, standing in the cold and packing Choc Wedges into boxes. Money was tight and I was sure to take advantage of the factory policy that allowed the staff to eat ice creams that were regarded as spoilt – especially the chocolate and nut combinations from the tops of Drumsticks that were regarded as misshapen and not fit for sale.

I have a lot to be thankful for when it comes to my parents' contribution to my life. In that second year at university, it wasn't really any easier for me. I had to work at my studies, manage distractions and it was dogged persistence that got me through. I had to learn resilience. Like so many qualities that people hold in high regard, resilience is something you need that doesn't necessarily come naturally: you have to acquire it consciously, through experience. I was a bit different in my family, and my mother, who had to take account of a lot of individual quirks among her 13 offspring, was always my friend. She would regularly back me up in my difference.

One important moment – important for me, at least – came during my Monash days when she helped me buy a motorcycle. Monash opened in 1961 in the new suburb of Clayton, 23 kilometres from Melbourne's city centre. Public transport links to the campus then were slow and unsatisfactory – and aren't much better today – and I needed transport. I couldn't afford a car and didn't really want one. I wanted a motorbike – but I couldn't afford one of those either.

I was going out with a bloke who had a motorbike and I put the case for a motorbike to my parents. This was essentially an outrageous proposition. First, the bike-riding boyfriend, then the idea of getting into leathers and being a motorcycle mama in my own right! Initially dad wasn't impressed, but luckily mum was more amenable. She had an inheritance from her father and from that she gave me $300 so that I could purchase a motorcycle, which I did – a Soviet-made, 350cc single-cylinder model called a Cossack.

I loved that bike – the whole experience of the leathers and the helmet and the freedom it gave me. And I loved my mum even more for backing me and winning the argument with my dad. I kept the motorbike through the rest of my time as a student and even used it during my first teaching assignment at Nhill High School in Victoria's Wimmera district until the distances from Melbourne and the northeast were just too long. I was being rebellious in wanting that motorcycle and my mother's timely support with money, understanding and empathy meant a great deal to me – they were characteristics I wanted to bring into my own life.

Her backing was crucial just a few years later too, when in my mid-20s, with some experience as a teacher under my belt and armed with the knowledge that I couldn't see a teaching career as my life's work, I returned to the idea of being a farmer. I'd earned a bit of money, been doing some travelling around the world and I knew that I wanted to farm. Being a farmer wasn't only about growing grass and looking after animals: I loved the ideal of rural living, in a community with that sense of interdependence that had characterised my upbringing. I was optimistic I could build a life based around practical outdoor work, earning enough off-farm income to support my community interests and travel.

I decided to buy a small farm in northeast Victoria, close to Albury–Wodonga where there was an airport and opportunities for off-farm work. I knew that it would have been folly to expect that I'd inherit my mum and dad's farm. I suspected there would be lots of interest from the others in the family and it would have meant a long wait. Having let that prospect go, I set about talking to mum and dad about being a farmer. A bit like the motorbike, my father had limited time for that idea. As far as he was concerned, girls were farmers' wives but never farmers. But my mother got it. She understood that I wanted to buy a farm, and because she'd come from a farm and she'd understood the sexism of her large family, with boys' roles and girls' roles, she became my chief backer.

This was truly an audacious step. Once my father understood my determination, he pretty much gave it his assent by default along the lines of 'Okay, well, you go off and buy yourself a farm'. But my mother took a steady and rather stealthy approach. Over a couple of years, she let her neighbours know I was interested in buying some land. The two of us started going farm shopping, checking out any farm that came on the market. But eventually, one of the landholders in the valley – a dairy farming family just like us but getting older – decided they wanted to sell their hill country and keep their flat country for their retirement. They didn't advertise it. Mum heard about it in the community network. She found my farm and helped me find the courage to buy it. And my parents helped me with the finance as well. The banks wouldn't give me a loan, so they acted as guarantors. In the end, the purchase became a family enterprise, with two of my brothers and one sister coming in with me to buy a larger piece of land that we later subdivided. So by 1980 I was single, aged 26, with an Arts degree, a Diploma of Education, a car, a farm and no house. I had direction in my life and I was excited about the possibilities.

Chapter 3

A WOMAN IN AGRICULTURE

I really did enjoy teaching. After two years at Nhill, I was pleased to come home, and taught legal studies at the Catholic senior secondary school, Galen College, in Wangaratta. It was exciting to be in that environment of Year 11 and 12 students getting ready to launch themselves into the world. Despite the joy I felt helping these students on their life's journey I did not see myself being a school teacher forever. Halfway through my first year, in 1978, I saw an advertisement in the local paper for a research assistant job in the office of the recently elected federal member for Indi, Mr Ewen Cameron. He was an old style, gentleman politician. As a mark of respect, I still address him as Mr Cameron. He was a Liberal, a farmer from Euroa who had won Indi in a three-cornered contest, defeating the incumbent, the National Party's Mac Holten, at the December 1977 election, with Labor Party preferences.

It looked like an interesting job. Mr Cameron did not know me but he knew my father through farming and Liberal Party connections. I interviewed for the position and he offered it to me. But the timing wasn't right; on reflection, I didn't want to abandon my Year 12 students with their exams only a few months away. I declined but asked him to keep me in mind if something came up in the future. It did, a little over a year later, when the person who took that researcher post moved on. This time, I said 'yes' and joined his office at the start of 1980.

I took the position not because I had any great affinity for the Liberal Party or the political mission of the government of Malcolm Fraser but because the work looked interesting and it was local. In no way did I imagine I was setting myself up for a parliamentary career. It turned out my instincts had been right: the job was great and, like so much of what I did subsequently, useful training for my future as an MP. I split my time between the electorate office in Wangaratta, where I worked with a secretary, Marg Dearing, and Mr Cameron's poky little parliamentary office in Canberra. With only two of us 'staffers' there was a lot to do, including researching Mr Cameron's speeches, managing the media contacts, handling constituent inquiries and drafting his correspondence.

Old Parliament House was a stimulating place to be around as well. Most importantly, I learnt about the business of being a local member and a legislator. I had the task of going through all the newspapers from within the electorate each week and compiling a file of cuttings that kept Mr Cameron informed about what was happening across Indi. And there were local policy issues to deal with. For example, the changing of the taxation arrangements on tobacco – something of great significance in Indi, which produced a good proportion of the national tobacco crop – had far reaching impacts on the economy, employment and community organisations.

Mr Cameron set a wonderful example of what a local politician should be. He was gentle, calm and respectful – a good man to work for. And he made sure he kept in touch with the people in his seat. He had a caravan that he would take around Indi and set himself up for a day in the towns and talk to the voters. Sometimes I went with him and I saw how much it meant to people just to feel that they'd been listened to by their Member of Parliament. It was fun, shuttling between Wangaratta and Canberra, but by the time the Fraser government fell to the Labor Party under Bob Hawke in March 1983, I was ready to move on. I had my farm, I was pushing 30, and while I'd learnt about how politics, the public service, the media and the legislature worked, I didn't want to get any deeper into that political existence. The life of the politician held no appeal, that was for sure. I knew what the job was. It was so demanding. I'd seen how hard Mr Cameron had worked – the relentlessness of it – and I didn't want that.

What I wanted was to be self-employed and try my hand at running my own consultancy using what I'd learnt while working for Mr Cameron, and, more importantly, to work within my community – and I knew even then that this required a long-term commitment.

Here's the thing about being a community-based politician: personal networks are everything, but you can't fake those connections or have an ulterior motive. It takes years to establish and nurture, and genuine motivation and integrity are key factors. Another recommendation worth making at this stage of the story is: never be afraid to talk to people and be willing to ask if you want to know how something works. That's not only because it's how to learn, it's how relationships are forged, and ultimately they're what count.

Our electorate office in Wangaratta was housed in a building that included other federal government services and departments. Next door to us was the Commonwealth Employment Service and the Department of Social Security. With some regularity, people would go into the CES or DSS with a problem and would then be directed to Mr Cameron's office. Often, if we couldn't help them, we'd send them to the social workers at the DSS. We established close working relationships with the people in the other Commonwealth departments. I made a lifelong friend in Alana Johnson, one of the social workers. We shared an interest in agriculture and community development and over the next three decades we worked on many projects together and Alana eventually followed me as the convenor of Voices for Indi. It was during this time that I came to understand how bureaucrats worked and how much can happen with good relationships. To that end, I learnt so much on those Friday afternoon coffee sessions in the staffroom where all the Commonwealth staff would get together, and in the years after, when I needed to know what was happening about some issue, I'd often ring up the colleagues that I'd met there. That was an early introduction to how goodwill and networking could produce information and outcomes.

One more observation that is relevant to my story: if you want to create change in your community, be willing to get formally involved in community organisations. I'm what American social theorists call a 'joiner'. I've served on all manner of boards and committees to do with education, community credit, the arts, health services, farming and the agricultural environment. They haven't always been leadership roles, either. Often, you can contribute to the collective leadership just by showing up and pitching in and doing whatever needs to be done. That's what happened with my early involvement with a group of like-minded women, and the establishment of Australian Women in Agriculture. Eventually, I would become national president and a life member but my first role was as the secretary and note taker – a post that generally attracts few volunteers in most organisations.

When I struck out on my own, setting up a consultancy business that sought to connect the community and local institutions with the bureaucracy and parliament, I was able to use my local involvement to produce some satisfying policy outcomes. I worked all around the region and often with local governments, planning for community services. I'd been an active volunteer and board member with the Murray River Performing Group, which was the mother body for the Flying Fruit Fly Circus, a circus for young people between eight and 19, based in Albury–Wodonga. With another consultant, I brought together the Victorian and federal governments to set up the Flying Fruit Fly Circus School. This combined normal school activities with circus training. Graduates of the Flying Fruit Flies now entertain crowds across the world, and the school still runs successfully 30-odd years later.

Another project was the design and winning of funding to establish a childcare service for farming families. It was a mobile service where the carers travelled to a community rather than care being based in a centre. It needed an innovative funding and organisational model in order to work within the regulations of two state and multiple local governments as well as with the Commonwealth, and the carers were all employed by the Albury–Wodonga education centre. It was satisfying work and wonderful to see the results deliver real benefits to rural families.

When it came along, the opportunity to work as a rural affairs advisor was hard to resist and in 1986 I accepted permanent work with the Victorian Department of Agriculture. This time I was working for a Labor government, led by John Cain. The job of the dozen or so rural affairs advisors around the state was to keep a Cabinet committee informed about what was going on in rural Victoria as well as organising committee meetings around the regions. This meant researching and writing briefing papers. There were some inspiring ministers, engaged, interested and principled, such as Evan Walker,

Kay Setches, Carolyn Hogg and Joan Kirner. I had enormous respect for Joan. She cared about the details and would send back briefs, telling us they weren't up to scratch and needed more work, and asking had we consulted widely enough, say, with the local women? I just loved that she wanted excellence from us. Working with the Department of Agriculture and Rural Affairs was such a positive experience and continued my education on learning how government works and how to get things done within government.

If people were complaining about funding for neighbourhood houses, the job was to make sure that the regional director of the neighbourhood houses met with the minister when they visited our district, prepare the brief, come up with recommendations and then follow through after the meeting, and ensure things would happen as a result. We had to be well-organised and solutions-focused and then use the good will of the public service and the political power of the government to effect change. The Cain government had a real commitment to regional Victoria and backed this with policy, a realistic budget and other resources.

With a change of government in the early 1990s, and Jeff Kennett as Premier, I wanted to get back to my independent life where I was more answerable to my community rather than to a government. And there was the farming thing. I'd had the land for almost 10 years but didn't have a home on it. As the 1980s drew to a close, and I prepared to go back into consulting, my mother started to push me hard. She challenged me: 'You're never going to be a farmer if you aren't living on your land'. I'd been talking about building a house and living there but hadn't done anything about it. She flat out told me she didn't think I was ever going to make it happen. I replied that it was all too hard as I didn't know what was happening in my life. Was I going to get married? Would I take on an international job perhaps? I loved travelling. But as a single woman, I could see designing and building a house just for myself and making the decision to base myself there would require a lot of energy. She kept challenging me, and I had to conclude that after 10 years I needed to face some truths and get on with building my farmhouse.

This was an opportunity for me to take advantage of my nature, being independent of spirit, not fitting the norm, able to make big decisions because I knew my own mind. I wanted to be true to myself and I wanted my house to reflect my values. The result was an off-grid, solid stone dwelling of irregular design, with room for visitors and self-sufficient in electricity and water. In 1991, when I moved in, I held a big housewarming party. The yard was festooned with fairy lights, my nieces and nephews formed a guard of honour on the path to the front door, and my mother gave a speech and officially opened the house by cutting a ribbon. There's a foundation stone nearby marking the moment. This was a turning point for me. I was now in my late 30s and I was settling into my life, comfortable with who I was. Until then, I'd been a wandering soul. But once I made the decision to settle, to be a farmer and to live on my farm, things fell into place. My mother's acceptance of who and what I was – a single woman farmer, a feminist, an independent person making my own living – encouraged me to make something truly meaningful of it.

And as I meshed my farming life with my consulting and community work, I started to fully comprehend the need not just to advance and promote the role of women in agriculture but for women's contribution to be widely recognised. I became heavily influenced by the inspiring feminist work of Marilyn Waring, a former conservative member of the New Zealand Parliament in the 1970s and 80s. She saw the discrimination against women not only in her own country but elsewhere in the world, including Australia, in which no dollar value was ever officially placed on the contribution made by women farmers to the national economy. She introduced me to feminist economics, a discipline I hadn't even been aware of. Gradually, my understanding of the importance of elevating women's economic contribution, particularly in agriculture, got me out and about in Australia, building my skills in running workshops and linking me with many national women's organisations, and, after a national campaign, successfully changing the way the Australian Bureau of Census and Statistics counted women's non-paid domestic and farming work.

My happy time living across the valley from both of my parents did not last long. My mother developed cancer and died in January 1993. This was another turning point. A few weeks later, I took part in a meeting of about 15 women to establish Australian Women in Agriculture – an organisation that continues to right the wrongs so accurately observed by Marilyn Waring as well as encourage more and more women to pursue independent careers on the land, whether it be in farming or in broader rural development activities. But I was incredibly sad for quite a while after mum died. She was only 65 and she left a gaping hole in our family. She was a loving, caring mother with strong opinions, particularly about social justice and fairness. I concluded that I couldn't afford to feel this way forever, so I needed to do something about it. I had to make another leap to avoid the sadness.

The leap I made was back to university. My sister Ruth was an extension officer with the Department of Agriculture and, at the urging of her employer, she had completed a master's degree in systems agriculture at the University of Western Sydney's Hawkesbury campus. She had become an enthusiastic advocate of the course and had been urging me to do it. As Ruth described it, 'This course is really good: it's practical, it's coursework, it's about rural community development, you'll love it. It's designed for people like us.' I'd waved her away initially – study had been so hard for me – but in the face of my sadness, I reconsidered my reluctance and enrolled. The course was a revelation, opening up a whole new set of perspectives. One of the take-home messages from that course was that your experience is real, and you have to understand that; you have to pay attention to what happens to you. If you have a really clear idea of your own experience, you can take the next step and compare that with other people's experience. You can talk to people and you can read theory, but it's your own experience that is real. Until then, I had downplayed my own life experiences, preferring to give greater credibility to those of other people – my sense of being 'other' had been strong – but I was slowly becoming more comfortable in my own skin. It was liberating.

This knowledge gave me a new sense of self-confidence. My time at Hawkesbury fundamentally changed me as well as developing my passion for rural and regional Australia. I met a lot of clever people who shared my interest, a whole department of them. When I challenged them about the lack of recognition of women in agriculture, they made me a member of the academic staff, and I was employed to teach the subject. I was the only female member of the faculty.

The experience of being a member of staff, initially at Hawkesbury and later at La Trobe University and Wodonga College of TAFE, coupled with being on the executive of Australian Women in Agriculture, deepened my interest in leadership and I went on to complete the Australian Rural Leadership Program. This 18-month experiential leadership course, which included a study trip to Asia and America, was life changing. It improved my leadership skills and confidence, gave me ample opportunity to exercise my courage muscle, rubbed off some rough edges on my leadership style and introduced me to a network of rural leaders with a shared vision for a prosperous and caring Australia alive with opportunities. The architecture of my life throughout my 40s and 50s was set in place. I became deeply involved in rural development, built up my consultancy in Australia and overseas and became part of many community and industry organisations, and advisory committees to all levels of government.

My father survived my mother by 19 years, dying in his late 80s in 2012. Dad had been sceptical about some of my choices early on. We had many discussions and arguments about agriculture and women's roles, but he eventually came around. Despite or maybe because of our differences, I loved him deeply. He was so proud when I became the national president of Australian Women in Agriculture and that I had developed my own business. He had been a founder of the Australian Institute of Agricultural Science, which in 2001 gave me an award for Excellence in Extension for the work I'd done in setting up 'Women and Dairy' discussion groups throughout the country. We travelled together to the award ceremony in Toowoomba, where he was surrounded by all his old colleagues. It was a great moment for both of us.

So now you have some idea of how I lived my life in the electorate of Indi until a Saturday night in May 2012, when I answered a phone call.

Chapter 4

A PHONE CALL

It was Saturday 12 May 2012. I was home and had a fire going. I was on my own, reading a book – I don't remember what it was – and was having a lovely, quiet night and thinking about whether I should get ready for bed soon. When the phone rang at 9.30pm, I was surprised; it was unusual to get a call after 8. On the line were my niece Leah Ginnivan and nephew Ben McGowan, calling from a terrace house in Melbourne's inner north. Like so many young adults from our district, they'd moved to the city for study, professional experience and work. One thing that often goes unrecognised is that rural and regional Australia's most valuable export is our young people. Leah and Ben sounded like they'd been having a good time, probably after a glass or two of wine had been consumed at a dinner party in their Fitzroy share house. But they had a serious proposition to put to me, which went along the lines of 'Cathy, we've been having dinner together and we think we need to make Indi a marginal seat and we reckon you should run as an independent candidate'.

When many of our young people from the northeast move to Melbourne, they set up households and even micro-neighbourhoods in the inner suburbs where they form mini expat communities. Naturally, the talk will turn to home and at this get-together Ben and Leah and a few others were bemoaning life in regional areas – how they weren't going to come home because there were so few opportunities on offer.

Their assessment was that, as things were, the situation in the valleys and towns of Indi was hopeless. They told me, 'The trains didn't work, there was little if any mobile phone coverage, no internet, few jobs and no-one cared about climate change!' Decades of voting faithfully for candidates put forward by the Liberal or National parties, making the seat safe for the Coalition, had not produced much of a return and they reckoned this shouldn't be allowed to go on.

I am known for being direct, and even with my nieces and nephews, who I love dearly, I could have been expected to have said, 'No, go away, talk to somebody else'. But I didn't. Instead, I said I thought it was an interesting idea and I would need some time to think it through. Two things lay behind this response. Four years earlier, in 2008, I had attended Kevin Rudd's 2020 Summit, an unjustly derided ideas-fest designed to look for ways to create a better Australia in the third decade of the 21st century. At the Summit, four keynote speakers on the first day were under 25, and they talked about their vision for Australia. I was stunned by their ability, by their level of articulation, by their creativity, their vision for Australia and the thought that they'd given to their presentations. My biggest takeaway from that Summit was that older people such as myself – and most of the attendees, in fact – needed to pay attention to the young people in our community.

They knew things that we Baby Boomers did not know. They were certainly better educated and had new approaches that could find the answers to the problems we were facing. It hit me like a tidal wave that the people in the industry and community organisations that I was part of, along with my social circle, were of a similar vintage to me. I made a firm commitment to pay attention and get to know the young people not only in my life but in my work. As a result, I expanded my consultancy business and took on two younger women as partners, and made a commitment to pay particular attention to my nieces and nephews. So when the phone call came through, I thought this was an opportunity to put that resolution into practice. What excited me was the opportunity to work with them in Melbourne, get to know them better – to hook into their energy and their views of the world.

The other factor prompting me to get involved was a sense of my mortality, sparked by my father's death only a month before I took that phone call. As I sat in the church in Wodonga for his funeral and listened to people talking about the story of dad's life, I was reminded in the most profound way that it comes to an end for all of us. My time was running out. I was 58. If I was going to get on with doing what I wanted to do in my life, now was the time. If I was to effect some meaningful change for the better, I had to start doing some serious work towards being the change I wanted to see.

I did not want to be the candidate as Leah and Ben had suggested. I was happy, well established in my career, settled in my relationships, and was not looking for any major disruptions. But I did agree with them. Something needed to be done. Sophie Mirabella had been the Liberal member for Indi since the 2001 election. She'd been re-elected in 2004, 2007 and 2010. Two Liberals had preceded her – Lou Lieberman and, of course, Mr Cameron. In fact, since 1931 Indi had bounced between the two Coalition parties. Indi was a safe seat, meaning the MP had won the seat without needing to go to preferences.

At the most recent election in 2010, Sophie's primary vote was 52.6 per cent, and after preferences were distributed she was on a margin of 9.9 per cent. While I thought winning the seat was pie-in-the-sky, I did want to test the feeling within the electorate, to see if it would be worthwhile challenging the Liberals. And if an independent campaign looked like it might be able to grow some legs, then someone needed to run in the seat. And I did want to work with these young people and learn from them, and their energy. I was also keen to assist them to be more engaged in the political and community-building process as part of the exercise as well. I could see it would be a project we could work on together and, even though it was going to take a huge amount of time, I thought, 'Well, it could lead to something positive – something people can build on'.

Despite my rather muted response to Leah and Ben and their friends and other young members of the extended McGowan clan, I was excited by the idea. I was thrilled that they had contacted me. It would be a challenge and I did know how to organise and strategise. That could be my contribution. I agreed to come to Melbourne to get things started. I rang what was to become my inner circle of trusted advisors, and asked their opinions. My sister Ruth, who lived in Gippsland, was a councillor and Mayor during the 2009 fires, knows about government, is an experienced leader and was interested in politics; David Wolfenden, my partner, a grain and sheep farmer living in southern NSW, is also a leader in agriculture and takes an active interest in national and state politics; Alana Johnson was a member and chair of a number of boards and had an intuitive feeling for community engagement. 'The young people have suggested this idea; what do you think, could it work, would you be interested?' Within a few weeks, talking it through with David, we agreed, we were up for this.

That first meeting in Melbourne was an extended family activity – several of my sisters and their children and friends turned up. Ruth put up sheets of butchers paper on the walls in this single-fronted Victorian terrace and ran a facilitated problem-solving and brainstorming process based on Edward de Bono's Six Thinking Hats. We analysed

A PHONE CALL

the voting trends in Indi using Australian Electoral Commission data. Over the 11 years since Sophie Mirabella had won the seat, the Liberal primary vote had fallen consistently. Sure, the seat was still safe but that 2010 primary vote of 52.6 per cent was 10 per cent lower than what she'd attracted just two elections earlier, in 2004. Given the trajectory, it would be possible to make the seat marginal. If we could get the preference flow in our favour. If we could get a great candidate. If we could mobilise a team of volunteers. If we could win Wodonga. So many 'ifs'. The meeting ended with a sense of absolute non-conclusion but a little glimmer of hope that this project might be worth working on.

Everyone put their hands up for a job. This was a presidential election year in America – Barack Obama was running for re-election – and one of the group, Cam Klose who had grown up in Yackandandah, had been to America and had written about the election campaign for the region's biggest newspaper, Albury's *Border Mail*. He was fascinated with the mechanics of campaigning and undertook to update himself on the sort of community campaigning methods Obama was using. The group, nicknamed 'the Indi expats', started meeting once a fortnight and I would regularly drive to Melbourne to take part.

Meanwhile, back home I called my colleagues and friends who I knew were unhappy with the way things were, told them about the agitation happening in Melbourne and asked if they'd like to 'do something'. Some of these were graduates of the Australian Rural Leadership Program including Alana, and others were graduates of the Alpine Valleys Community Leadership Program, colleagues from my days working in the Department of Agriculture, and importantly members of our farmers' organisation Australian Women in Agriculture. Subsequently, two months after the terrace house meeting,

12 of us met at the library in Wangaratta and gauged the level of interest in doing something political. Fortunately, this older cohort was keen to explore the idea and committed to meeting every two weeks as well. By September, Voices for Indi was born and I had accepted the role of convenor.

One of the things that motivated us was our sense that Indi had been taken for granted and we wanted to change that. The seat takes in Victoria's snowfields and mountains, including eight major rivers capturing 52 per cent of the water in the Murray–Darling Basin. In the north are the larger urban centres of Wodonga and Wangaratta, and it runs as far south as Kinglake and Marysville, towns that were devastated in the 2009 Black Saturday bushfires. We knew that other regional centres such as Ballarat, Geelong and Bendigo have historically been in marginal federal and state electorates. Even the seat of Gippsland, which contains Traralgon, looked like going marginal after the 2007 election, which gave the National Party a real fright. Being in a competitive, marginal seat makes a big difference. The political activity can generate more economic activity in a seat and lead to bigger and more diverse populations. And more train connections. Bendigo, for example, has 24 separate train trips a day to Melbourne; in Albury–Wodonga there are four. There were many advantages to being a marginal seat, and not many in being a safe seat.

What was it about our community that we wanted to change? In a later chapter I will outline the results of our major communication consultation – the Indi 'kitchen table conversations' – and in these early days the major issues people talked about were the level and type of representation, lack of mobile phone coverage, poor if any internet, lack of public transport, costs of fuel and energy, and the isolation which made access to services, education and employment difficult and expensive.

Northeastern Victoria is not poor in the sense of being poverty-stricken, but it is poor in the sense that it does not have a lot of inherited, property-based wealth like, say, farmers of Victoria's Western district. It's also poor in services in the sense that, relative to the other regional centres, it's further away from Melbourne, which is the epicentre of public services. Although these are not acute problems in Wodonga and Wangaratta, which were more suburbanised and had greater economies of scale, in other parts of Indi the cost of living was high. But people made do and did not mind too much because the communities and family networks are strong. But there was definitely a progressive feeling of being forgotten in the years Sophie Mirabella became ensconced as the federal member after 2001.

The maintenance of the train line, which is part of the rail connection between Melbourne and Sydney, was a massive issue and remained so all through my time as an MP. I regarded this as a huge failure of government, chiefly through neglect. The replacement of wooden sleepers between Melbourne and Albury with concrete ones in 2011 had not worked out and meant that trains often had to travel slowly, meaning they regularly ran late. The carriages were old. The level of community discontent and unhappiness about their train was huge.

Another big issue was poor telecommunications. Telstra, as the major provider, built mobile phone towers where they were guaranteed to get a lot of use; that is, in towns not rural areas. Indi's valleys hosted very few towers, making mobile phone coverage patchy. This is unacceptable at any time but especially so given that northeastern Victoria is one of the most bushfire-prone places in the world.

A third issue, which was not so much a hot button among voters but was definitely one that needed attention and contributed to the lack of opportunities in our area, was how poorly we scored in terms of post-school education and training. For example, 22 per cent of people nationally have a tertiary qualification but in Indi the number was 14 per cent.

During my work with the Office of Rural Affairs and in my consultancy business I had seen these symptoms of rural decline in many communities. I had also experienced the impact that rigorous policy, resources, community action and leadership could make.

When a community continually misses out on opportunities, this can become a self-fulfilling process because more and more people feel disconnected from the political and bureaucratic systems. As I talked to people about the issues, I'd ask, 'Why don't we do something about mobile phone coverage, or the train, or mental health?' It wasn't that people weren't innately clever – many were and are – but a special type of knowledge is needed to tackle the major telcos. Similarly, if an area isn't growing, and it isn't becoming more educated, isn't attracting more people or making substantially more money, then its ability to innovate and change lags too. This was what had happened to our area compared with the regional towns in many other parts of the state. It couldn't go on like this.

I could see that we had these key issues that were increasingly sensitive in our region and a vulnerable sitting member. There was a sense of the community's patience running out as far as the status quo was concerned; the decline in the Liberals' primary vote showed that. But such things are only the preconditions; only action can lead to achievement. It was at this point that we were able, as the community group Voices for Indi, to put to work so much of what we had learnt about community and leadership. 'Think global, act local' is another political cliché, but like many clichés it has a basis of truth.

It's easy to be overwhelmed by all the problems in the world. But over the years I had come to believe that the best, most effective way to have an influence on these global issues was to act within my sphere of control. This was an idea developed in a book by Stephen Covey, *The Seven Habits of Highly Effective People*, which many of us had been introduced to during the days of our Leadership Programs. You begin with yourself – my attitudes and behaviours – and again here comes a cliché, be the change I want to see. If I stay true to myself, I am in control of what I do. This gives me a sense of personal power that enables me to work on and with others, growing my circle of influence. Slowly, the circles expand and become a community 'movement'. For me, working with community was never an escape; it was the most important place to begin in order to be effective.

What ran through my head during the second half of 2012, as our group of young Indi expats in Melbourne and Voices for Indi in the northeast talked about how we might create change in Indi, was the importance of a community-focused strategy.

This theory of change wasn't only theoretical knowledge. My whole personal leadership philosophy was based on community leadership. I'd seen the power of community engagement when working with Women in Agriculture on counting women's work in the Census. I'd seen it when introducing new arrangements in the Ovens Valley around the tobacco tax. I'd seen it working in projects supported by the Office of Rural Affairs in reinventing small rural towns.

When I wanted to be a farmer, I couldn't get a loan because women farmers weren't taken seriously. As women farmers we couldn't get recognition for our role in agriculture. Working to improve service delivery for farming families, we were blocked by the lack of a regional development policy at government level. My experience, our experience, was clear: if we were to effect change, we needed to speak up, organise, have solutions to problems, engage with the power structures and institutions, learn the rules of the game and use them. We needed strategies at every level. We had to learn to find our voices and learn to be heard.

My past work in groups and on committees taught me to have action – you need activity. You need to envisage and plan, allocate resources, establish priorities and decide what actions must be taken. These lessons can come from anywhere. I had been part of the Indigo Valley Landcare Group, which had a community plan to get rid of blackberry infestations. As a committee we developed the plan under the guidance of a skilled facilitator and invited all the interested landowners to be part of the planning and strategy. We set up processes for engaging and winning farmers' and neighbours' support and cooperation, and organised a community barbecue, creek walks and site visits. We discussed and got agreement on what was needed, and then set about implementing the plan over a two-to-five-year period. In the early days my role was to publish the local newsletter; communication was essential to motivate people not just to buy into the plan but also to engage in the activities required to bring it into effect.

A key element had to be to keep everyone informed, and to be open to hearing other, often dissenting ideas. Later, when I was elected as the president of the Landcare Group, some of the older, wiser people in the community mentored me in how leadership worked at the community level. As president, I was the figurehead, the appointed spokesperson, yet I was also just one among equals. It was essential everyone respected the various roles that needed to be performed to get to where we wanted to go. From this, I came to see that, to maximise community engagement and participation, there needed to be clarity about the task, the time frame and the resources that were required. And finally, as always – fun celebrations and recognition when the task was completed.

In community groups and committees, it's easy to find yourself engaged in work that keeps you busy but is not really effective. The big challenge is to get agreement on what is success – what Covey called 'beginning with the end in mind'. A good discipline is to remain mindful that volunteer time is a scarce resource, so you need to use it wisely. Another lesson to learn as a community leader, if you hold a leadership position or find yourself in a role where others look to you for guidance, is how important it is to genuinely consult. A top-down or do-as-I-say model may look more efficient, but if you're patient and set aside the necessary time, resources and skills, and consult, engage and encourage participation, a community can achieve big things, as we were to prove in Indi.

There is another element to community action that's often underrated or misunderstood: courage. It's common to view courage solely as an individual characteristic but it can exist in a group. It's also seen as something that is innate: either you have it, or you don't. I see it differently.

The thing I know about courage is that the more you use it – the more you speak your truth, act your truth, do what you think is the right or the best thing – the less scary something becomes. The more familiar you become with its use, the more confident you can feel in backing your own judgment. Does the fear of failure and humiliation ever go away? No, but as you get familiar with exercising your courage muscle, the easier it becomes to manage that fear. The months we spent thinking about how we would go about trying to make changes in Indi were exciting but also informed by trepidation. Slowly, slowly we were growing our courage muscle. I do not believe we are born with abundant courage. Courage is a muscle. It exists within all of us perhaps in some small way, but each of us has to learn how to use it, to work on it, exercise it, build it up.

As we contemplated running a candidate at the 2013 election, it became increasingly evident that there was so much to know about the raw practicalities of politics. The current MP for Indi was an astute political operator, one of the very few women frontbenchers in Tony Abbott's shadow cabinet. Putting someone up against her would be tough. We needed guidance. Fortunately, there was someone to turn to – a lifetime savvy politician who had served in the New South Wales and federal parliaments for many years and had scaled the heights: former deputy prime minister Tim Fischer.

Judy Brewer, my cousin, is married to Tim, but he was much more than a family connection. We had enjoyed a long professional relationship. As minister for trade in the late 1990s, Tim had been a great supporter of the work of Australian Women in Agriculture. As president of the organisation I had worked closely with him on issues including the introduction of the GST, trade agreements and organising international conferences. And a few years later, while I was teaching at the University of Western Sydney, I accompanied Tim, who had retired from politics, on a trade mission to Iran.

In November 2012, I had a meeting with Tim to tell him about our ideas for Voices for Indi. Tim and Judy were living on her farm in Mudgegonga, right in the middle of Indi, and he was interested in knowing what I was up to. It's important to stress that Tim is 100 per cent loyal to the National Party and in no way did I want to compromise him. I also knew, because of the Coalition agreement, that the Nationals were not running a candidate in Indi and I thought he may have some insights that could be helpful.

I told him about the formation of Voices for Indi, that we were planning a community development consultation process across the electorate and hoping to find a candidate. Later, I sent this note of the meeting to our group: 'Tim said be upfront with Sophie. Meet with her, give her a one-page letter describing what we're doing. If she knows about it from us before she finds out from others, she won't be able to come out afterwards and say she didn't know about it, be cross and stroppy. Plus, being open with her fits with our values of being transparent, open and honest.' When Tim suggested that, it was the last thing that any of us wanted to do.

The note went on: 'He didn't think the Liberals would throw lots of money at Indi, and even if they did, he thinks that Sophie would be too proud to accept it. She would see it as a threat, particularly if we maintain a very low-key community focus. In terms of publicity he thought that the webpage and using word-of-mouth to get out [our message] would be a good thing.' He also talked about the importance of early meetings with local media including Di Thomas, the editor of *The Border Mail*, and other regional newspapers to brief them of our plans, with a view to having a news story published before Christmas. This would mean that over the holiday period people would be able to talk about Voices for Indi during social gatherings, and the low-key seeding of community conversation about another approach to politics could begin. He was looking at this strategically, which was a great help.

He asked about the candidate and said he didn't think it mattered that we didn't have a 'hero' to put forward at that stage. A low-key start, building community involvement, was a good approach, he believed, and it would keep us off the political radar so that we could announce the candidate with a big fanfare in May. He thought that would be about the right time and agreed a transparent selection process was a priority. He called this a 'creep up' campaign, in which we did not start out loudly, but crept up into the electorate's consciousness. We followed his advice, including the meeting with Sophie and various editors.

I requested a meeting with Sophie soon after and received an email reply: 'Dear Cathy, Sophie would be available to meet you at 5 p.m. in her Wangaratta office on Wednesday the 19th December 2012'. I was joined in that meeting with Voices for Indi member Tony Lane. The meeting lasted 11 minutes. We told Sophie about Voices for Indi, a community-inspired organisation, and outlined our purpose and desire for improved representation. We told her about the unrest in the electorate, about our intention to run a community-wide consultation as part of the process and that we would send her a copy of the results afterwards, which we did. We were upfront, just as Tim had suggested we should be. Sophie was polite, thanked us for letting her know and told us she didn't think we'd get anywhere because people in Indi weren't interested in politics. Both Tony and I left with the feeling that we wanted to test that assumption.

Chapter 5

SOMEONE HAS TO DO IT

How does a political novice get caught up in what with hindsight was one of the most bitter periods of federal battles in the history of Australian politics?

I have always been a political agnostic. True, when I left teaching I worked for a Liberal MP. But I later worked directly – and very happily – for a state Labor government and then did consultancy work for governments of both persuasions. For as long as I can remember, I've seen politics – with a small 'p' – as being about people and communities rather than parties or 'sides', about outcomes ahead of partisan positions and point-scoring. In 2012, it was clear even to me that the federal Labor government under Julia Gillard would not survive the next election. She was under siege from the man she replaced, Kevin Rudd, who wanted his job back, and the opposition leader Tony Abbott. I didn't like Abbott's way of politics. It was hard and brutish. I thought he lacked respect. He was determined to turn back the clock on dealing with climate change, which as a farmer I thought lacked logic and as a businesswoman I regarded as irresponsible. And his 'stop the boats' rhetoric was excessive and alarmist, lacking mercy, charity and love. I definitely couldn't see how his positions could improve the lives of my fellow electors in Indi.

With my background and interests, I should have been an enthusiastic supporter or even a member of the National Party. I wasn't because it didn't represent the rural and regional Australia I knew, which was diverse and made up of more than people who owned farms or mines.

The National Party seemed to me to be overwhelmingly male and old. It didn't have a coherent strategy on regional development – no vision of what it wanted the regions to look like. In my leadership roles with Australian Women in Agriculture and my consulting work, I'd been advocating about women's issues, childcare and adult education and the importance of communication, transport and services. Some of these issues seemed to be irrelevant to the men in the National Party, so that party wasn't for me. I felt that Labor was basically an urban party, and increasingly the Greens became an urban party too, fighting for Labor votes. Come election time it was difficult for me to work out how to vote because too few candidates reflected the interests that were close to my heart. Interestingly, I found myself cautiously optimistic when Sophie won preselection in 2001. She was a young, single professional woman, with a law degree, obviously ambitious and keen to make a mark; could she be the change we needed in Indi? I was open to give her the benefit of the doubt.

But by 2012, the jury was in, and obviously I wasn't alone in my disappointment. But just how to go about shaking things up enough to give Sophie and the Liberals a fright by making the seat marginal was a contentious issue within our group right from the start. And the issue of how much we should concentrate on the citizen engagement and community development side of things as against straight-up, conventional political campaigning had to be negotiated from the beginning and in fact all the way through my time as a candidate and MP.

Some people in our team were traditional party people and they were used to campaigning as a top-down model. The other group, which included me, believed we could run a campaign that started at the grass roots, building community hubs, creating engagement and participation – more of a bottom-up approach. We had to find a way to accommodate both streams of thought; we certainly needed each other. The campaign group, for example, did the sensible, normal exercise of putting together a budget, working out how much money we would need to raise. We didn't know exactly how we were going to get the money but we were disposed towards relying on a large number of small donations rather than looking out for big donors – and this was how it would play out in the next six years.

By November 2012, we had all come together and agreed on a philosophical approach and drafted a strategic plan, with a vision, desired outcomes, budgets, actions and teams – a solid look at who we were and what we wanted to achieve. Our values stated in that document are worth recalling, because they underpinned everything we did in the years ahead: 'Voice for Indi is committed to encourage a diversity of voices and opinion and participation in the electoral process. It's committed to ensuring that our electorate voice is heard and represented at the national level. It's committed to encouraging respectful and mature representation of our democratic voices. It's committed to undertake activities which will create an invitation to participate in our democracy. It's committed to developing and using simple elegant processes when engaging with the electorate. And Voices for Indi is committed to being honest and respectful, to being well informed and to referring to reputable sources when making statements.' These values still guide me and my approach to politics and I continually strive for elegant processes.

Voices for Indi continued to refine ways in which we could organise ourselves. Just prior to meeting with Sophie to talk about our issues,

Alana and I led an Australian Women in Agriculture delegation on a 10-day trip to India. We had been making trips to India, meeting women farmers, for several years. This trip ended up serving as an informal brainstorming session for Voices for Indi. Alana was already active in Voices for Indi as were a couple of other women on the trip. As we travelled around by bus, we workshopped how to run a community-engagement program around politics in northeastern Victoria. By the time we got back from India, we had designed a clear process for the implementation of what became known as kitchen table conversations. The kitchen table conversations model built on community engagement work done by the Victorian Women's Trust as part of the Purple Sage and Watermark projects, in which many members of Australian Women in Agriculture had participated.

As the calendar flipped over into January 2013, having got the movement going we still needed to find a candidate. The problem was that we couldn't get any serious takers. The Indi expats, the youngsters, kept telling me that I'd have to stand but I wasn't quite convinced to drastically change my life at this stage. We moved on with putting together kits for hosts and participants for the kitchen table conversations, which we scheduled to run through February and March. Our plan was to compile a report of everything we'd learnt and share it widely through the electorate in May. On January 30, Julia Gillard unwittingly did us an enormous favour by announcing that the election would be held in September. It was a gift. We could announce our candidate in May as we launched our Voices for Indi report and then have four months to campaign.

In February, we had initial meetings in community venues, neighbourhood houses and halls in Wodonga, Wangaratta, Benalla and Mansfield. We put the word around to people we knew, personal phone calls and group emails, inviting everyone to be part of a conversation about our community and representation. As team leader of this process, I explained how it would work, often called the snowball model. The people who wanted to attend (and dozens showed up) would invite family and friends to come to a comfortable convenient venue – it could be an office or a meeting room or their home, or even literally the table in their kitchen – for a one-hour meeting, with food, where attendees would be asked to answer a handful of questions: What do you love about northeast Victoria? What do you want out of a representative? What are your issues? Each host was provided with a kit which explained the process and expectations as well as form sheets to return information and data.

At these larger initial meetings, we ran the kitchen table process with the hosts, setting them up in groups at tables and asking them to answer the questions, so that they would have an experience of how the conversations should operate. Then over afternoon tea or supper, we would debrief: How was it? What had worked? How would they go running the conversations themselves? This process was in keeping with the experiential learning that I'd learnt at Hawkesbury. If you experience something with someone guiding you through, it's going to have a greater impact than if someone just tells you what to do and sends you off.

After participating in a briefing session, the hosts would run their own kitchen table conversations. I'd follow up later with a personal phone call, a chance to debrief and ask the hosts to get the material back to us by April. We had more than 50 hosts, and when you think about the word-of-mouth effect of them letting all the people in their networks know what we were doing, as well as the actual participants of the conversations, you can see the multiplier effect working away nicely. And some of those people were the ones who, when we wanted to get into the campaign, came with us on the journey.

I knew we were onto something when we had our second meeting for the hosts. We had worked hard to publicise the information evenings, advertising them in the local papers and working our personal contacts. In Wangaratta, over 30 people showed up and there was such enthusiasm in the room; I was a little stunned by how much people wanted a change. The people who showed up to these meetings weren't young, they were mostly middle-aged and older – reasonably conservative in their ways – but they were fired up. To a certain extent, we had to dampen that enthusiasm or at least try to redirect it. We had made it plain that these meetings weren't designed to produce a candidate, nor were we looking for a shopping list of issues. We wanted to stimulate community engagement and participation and to encourage people to use their voices.

Unlike traditional campaigns, we were not doing a survey or running a focus group. Instead we were testing our idea of a community-based campaign that would not be built around a 'star' candidate or a political party with a formal manifesto and a branch structure. We genuinely wanted to know what issues they cared about. We were also looking for ways to mobilise people for a future campaign. All of us were connected to our community through our work, our commercial relationships, our churches if we attended them, our friendships, our families, so we had a reasonable feel for the accuracy of the information coming back to us. That's how the model worked, and we applied it again in the lead-up to the 2016 election as well.

At these host meetings, I was the person up front talking about the process. As the meetings moved around the electorate, the discussion about ideal representation became increasingly fraught because we didn't actually have anyone who wanted to be the candidate. But by the time we'd conducted the first six meetings, the general response was summed up along these lines: 'This is such a good idea and we need to do this. Cathy, it ought to be you who runs.'

At the time, what we were doing did not seem remarkable. Alana and I and others in the team had often rolled out this sort of activity in fields requiring community or stakeholder engagement but we had never done it in a political space. Our thinking was that we were using a democratic process and a structure that resembled in a very loose way a political party in that we were setting up hubs rather than local branches. Within Voices for Indi, some of those interested in more traditional campaigns were saying that we were striking out and creating a new form of politics, but as far as I was concerned we were reframing political activity by redefining and updating community participation. I believed then and still do that the electoral system was designed for our way of working but the conventional parties had basically lost that understanding.

When I was elected, politicians from the major parties would tell me how amazed they were by our victory, which was flattering, but I was more disappointed that they didn't truly understand what we had done. Occasionally, I would suggest that they should do what we had done because, really, we weren't even doing anything especially novel. If the National Party did just half of what we did in regional and rural Australia and then represented through their policies what their communities told them, there would be many more National Party MPs. My belief is that we were simply making democracy work: that the person who got elected was representing the beliefs of the majority of people in that seat as they related to the lives, aspirations and environment of those electors. The representative would represent the people and the two would report back to each other. Surely this is the idea behind participatory democracy and our party system. Sadly, through the decades, it has slipped a long way from that.

While these conversations were going on with the older cohort, I still had to maintain my commitment to keep working with and energising the younger people, who were feeling especially left out. Young people were never great ones for the kitchen table conversations. Early on, I tried to get the Indi expats to meld into the adult committee but it was fraught. We would try to have Skype meetings of both groups at 10am on a Saturday, with us in Wangaratta and them in Melbourne, and it was challenging. Eventually we worked out a way of working, together and by distance, that suited most of us, based around a system of delegations and self-organising teams, with the expats largely taking responsibility for our social media operation and the software systems.

There were other lessons in how to get young people involved. During the campaign I was put in touch with a Year 12 student, a friend of one of the expats, and arranged to meet after school at our Wangaratta office. When she didn't show, I called her and she explained that she had been too scared to come and didn't want to be involved in Politics. I understood and explained that she was going to be voting for the rest of her life, and suggested we meet somewhere for a cup of coffee.

When we got together, she told me she didn't want to mess up her Year 12 studies or be regarded as a nerd, but in the conversation she revealed that marriage equality was a policy she was passionate about. She said if I committed to arguing for marriage equality, she would come to a meeting and bring two friends. I had no problem with doing that, although I wasn't sure Indi voters would feel well-disposed to this. It wasn't an issue that had come up in our kitchen table conversations. Anyway, she later brought her two friends and we had a good talk about marriage equality and during the campaign they got their friends involved and they made a number of clever short videos declaring their backing for me and shared them widely among their networks. That social networking of those young people was superb. It delivered a deep penetration into their demographic and, once I realised that working one-on-one with young voters was the way to find out about their issues, I added that to my toolkit.

All the time I was a Member of Parliament, I made a point of actively seeking out young voters. I understood that they weren't going to jump hurdles to help me do my job – I actually had to jump the hurdles if I wanted their input. By my final year in parliament, over 200 of Indi's young people took part in a series of breakfasts and online surveys, sharing their views and suggestions around the federal Budget. And by the way, I need not have worried about how Indi voters would react to my support of favouring marriage equality. In the 2017 plebiscite, 63 per cent of those who voted favoured it too.

We had something deeper than a simple set of learnings supporting us as we established Voices for Indi. Many of us had also worked together and had trust in each other's organisational ability. We had the skills and we had the networks. What enabled us to go from a dinner party idea to a fully-fledged, politically competitive community movement inside a year was that we built on these networks. They were social, industrial and familial. Shared interests and experiences, such as involvement in leadership programs and agricultural and community groups, figured strongly in the early iteration of Voices for Indi.

Participating in the Australian Rural Leadership Program had opened my eyes to the power of community leadership and opportunities to step up into leadership roles. In northeast Victoria there were a number of graduates who shared a vision for rural Australia and we stayed in contact, offering support and inspiration. Running in tandem was a popular community skills-based leadership program, the Alpine Valleys Community Leadership Program. In 2011 the combined northeast graduates of both programs hosted a national leadership conference in Beechworth which included international speakers. In the local context, this conference was a big event. And if you add the expertise of Australian Women in Agriculture, this meant there were plenty of people throughout Indi who knew how to organise and run events.

However, the Voices for Indi team was more than a collection of leadership graduates: it was a diverse group covering many skill sets, had connections to many organisations and as a result was very strong. We knew we weren't just diving into a fight. This was much bigger. The key question we wanted to address was 'Assuming that you want to represent and consult with your community, how do you do this in a way that's meaningful?' In Australia we don't as a rule consult well on any topic. Across the nation, our engagement processes are poor. Many Australians aren't familiar with their civic duty to engage in politics. Others are, but because the returns are often so poor they give up. As a result, we do not get the benefit of having governments that have a close connection with their communities. And that means governments and communities do not get the opportunity to work together.

One good recent example of how that can lead to bad policy outcomes is the 2017 Robodebt fiasco, in which the Coalition government made 470,000 unlawful demands on 373,000 welfare recipients for supposed overpayments. The cost of this disaster, which went on for years, approached the $1 billion mark. This showed how far removed from people the government had become. Thousands of Australians were telling the government that they had not been overpaid but the government told them they were wrong. The people weren't. What has happened in our system? When did the government stop listening?

Something similar happened in Indi when the Turnbull government changed the funding rules for mobile and rural childcare services in 2018. When the government introduced the changes, I argued ferociously against them because I could see it was going to have a huge negative impact on rural and regional Australia including the mobile childcare service we had set up in Albury–Wodonga. I unsuccessfully moved amendments in the parliament, organised deputations, even got the minister, Simon Birmingham, to come to Albury–Wodonga so that people at the local centres could present their case. They explained to him why the new rules wouldn't work in our area. He assured them things would be okay. That is, that they, the community, had it all wrong. Sure enough, once the changes went through, our local mobile childcare services collapsed, just as the minister had been warned. Our policy makers have got themselves to a regrettable place, where they aren't sufficiently close to communities to trust them to know their own best interests.

Voices for Indi were trying to remedy that, and a big step we took, after conducting the first round of kitchen table conversations, was to put the results together in a 16-page report that we released in May 2013. By this time, we had a logo and short-form moniker: V4I. Across 13 pages of that report, we published every word that had come from the people who had answered our kitchen table questions, without any value judgment. We wanted to make sure everybody could find their words there and we didn't try to come up with a little, hard summary or give any larger meaning to it; we were saying 'Here's what we've heard'. It was all there – thousands of words about living in Indi, about issues of concern, about what constituted a community and effective political representation. It was a way of showing voters that we already had a strong community; all we had to do was recognise that and harness ourselves to it in the four months between then and election day. We sent it to as many people as we could find. The intention was to flood the electorate with it.

Our Voices for Indi report had taken four months from conception to execution. Out of all the issues, and there were many, we took five that we thought we could do something about and used them for the campaign. At no stage did we commit to do everything suggested during the kitchen table conversations. We committed to listen, to represent and give voice.

For all of the value that the process delivered, it didn't do everything that we had hoped it would. I think that we had hoped we could naturally transform the people who'd come to the kitchen table conversations into activists, but it didn't work like that. The word-of-mouth side of it – the build-up of trust in our system, and getting Voices for Indi out into the community and raising our profile in the areas we needed to – worked. But it did not convert the people into Voices for Indi cadres, apart from some who had already hosted kitchen table conversations.

What it taught me was that it takes a long time to build a culture of political engagement; that a one-off experience was not enough to inspire a large number of people to say they were going to change, which ultimately was what we were asking them to do in this rural community. I learnt that even when things are going well and you've softened the ground, allowing you to build a brand, that's only the beginning of the work required for people to become politically active.

This lesson was like gold for me. Looking back, I can see we were perhaps too optimistic and perhaps a little bit naïve. I expected that our process would get them interested and they would say, 'Oh this is fascinating. I love it, I want to be involved, oh yes, participation's great.' Perhaps 500 did, which was probably a big number, but out of more than 110,000 people in the whole electorate it's not necessarily that many. In my time as a candidate and MP, the important thing to me was to understand that on the bell curve of people's interests it's very easy, in the role of an independent, to focus on the people who are active supporters. But that cannot be enough.

By the end of my second term, I had 20,000 people on my Facebook account. Most of the time I was probably working with about 8,000 active people on my social media. I knew that in Indi there were about 50–60,000 people in the middle of the political interest curve with a vague interest in politics or the activities of their representative, and then there was a significant tail who had no interest. I learnt, as I spoke to the hosts during our briefing sessions, what a hard thing we were asking people to do, which was to become politically involved. The kitchen table conversations proved to be a very safe way of starting.

Looking at that first report, we compiled a list of the key issues, and it was a very long list and one that suggested some negligence. When asked 'What are the practical issues within the Indi electorate that concern you?', the most frequently raised issues were transport and connectivity, roads and the train, access to broadband, better mobile phone reception, health services (especially affordable and available for an ageing population), mental health services, the future of agriculture, supply and use/reuse of water, climate change, the impact on food production, increased fires, the state of the natural environment, access to the NBN, employment opportunities, youth employment and the competitiveness of industries; then, the treatment of refugees and availability of funding for local government. The Indi expats had been spot-on in their analysis.

It confirmed for me the problem for Indi: there was never enough money. We had eight and a quarter local government jurisdictions, six with areas of State and National Parks, so these councils didn't have a large rate base and were always struggling to balance their budgets. While the problems were clear, the solutions were less so; how would we get better funding for local government so that it could deliver better services and build infrastructure? Local councils were responsible for many services including roads, aged care, home and community care, childcare and libraries. Clearly there was a structural fault at work and we needed to find a way to improve the system. One simple way would be to shift Indi out of the safe-seat column so that our voices could be heard for the first time in a long time. Indi was getting by, but unless there was a change it wasn't going to be able to break free, find a way to move up to the next level and improve lives. And we had to campaign to make that happen.

Chapter 6

THE CANDIDATE

The search for a candidate proceeded through the early months of 2013 without getting very far. A lot of people wanted a footballer: Mac Holten had played for Collingwood in the Victorian Football League and for Wangaratta in the Ovens and Murray League. But there were no takers.

Then the search shifted to finding someone known at the local level, with name recognition, like a mayor. I was known in agricultural and rural circles, and quite a few people knew my relatives, if they didn't know me. With such a large and extended family the McGowan name was well known in the northern end of the seat. I wasn't as well known in the south closer to Melbourne, but I'd served on boards, taught at the Wangaratta Catholic school, and met or worked with a lot of people in the region.

During the kitchen table conversations, I'd grown more comfortable with the idea of running. I'd never dreamed of being a parliamentarian, but this wouldn't be a hindrance. I thought, 'Well someone's got to do something'. A lot of people had been telling me they wanted me to do it, so in the end I was happy to say 'yes'. After all, I thought it wasn't as if we were going to win; it would just be a finite and relatively brief period of campaigning and then I could go back to my work.

However, the decision was a long time in the gestation. While initially I had rejected the idea of being the candidate when proposed by the Indi expats, I liked the general idea of creating some disruption in what had become a staid and dysfunctional electorate – upsetting the dominant paradigm had its attractions. That sounded like a worthwhile project to support. I was in. But could I see myself as a candidate? There were two conflicting elements at play: my reluctance to be the person out front in what I suspected would be a fierce battle versus the attraction of the opportunity to test our theories of community engagement and empowerment.

The process of the kitchen table conversations helped me realise that the Voices for Indi team and the Indi expats had developed a clear idea of how we might do this. By March 2013 it was obvious there was strong community support for action, to stop beating about the bush with process and do this thing we had been talking about. On the family front the young ones had been subtly and constantly egging me on to walk the walk, to step up, to be the change I wanted to see, and it had an impact. And truly, I didn't want to let them down. They and Voices for Indi had invested so much time and energy and taken big risks in getting us to this place.

In my work life, I thought the timing might also be suitable. I was managing two contracts, one in PNG in partnership with Charles Darwin University and the PNG Women in Agriculture Development Fund and the other with Australian Wool Innovation setting up women in wool groups. There were two other projects in the wings: with Alana and Australian Women in Agriculture we were negotiating with India to host the 5th International Conference of Women in Agriculture, but it was not progressing well; and planning for the fourth in a series of conferences for Connecting Rural Business Women. I discussed the idea with my colleagues and partners, and all agreed they could manage and actively encouraged me to step up.

THE CANDIDATE

Finally, I contacted my mum's brother who with his family lived in Rutherglen and had been involved in civic life for more than 60 years, and asked if he thought our idea could work. He gave me the go ahead. 'Why not? There's nothing to lose,' he said and, because I was driving my father's old Mercedes, suggested I get another car – 'preferably a Holden or a Ford; rural people pay attention to the car you drive'.

With the saying 'If not now, when?' ringing in my ears, I made the decision. I resigned from the position as convenor of Voices for Indi, rearranged my business and community affairs, and began the process of reconciling myself to six months of campaigning.

Running parallel to the kitchen table conversations, Voices for Indi established a subcommittee to work through a process for supporting a candidate who would commit to the ideals and actions outlined in the material gathered in the kitchen table conversations and Voices for Indi report. An advertisement was placed in regional papers calling for anyone interested in standing to meet with a subcommittee. Four people responded and two were interviewed. I was one of the two interviewees. The objective of this process was that it would allow Voices for Indi to say it supported the chosen person's campaign. My interview was tough, with the subcommittee members going out of their way to avoid any indication of favouritism or inside knowledge. I made my case and waited for the decision. It wasn't until May, at the launch of the Voices for Indi report, that I announced as an independent candidate running with the support and backing of the Voices for Indi team, committed to its ideals, behaviours and values. And our colour was orange.

Early on, I took care to maintain a grip mentally, keeping my bearings so as to avoid making the worst choice that aspiring politicians regularly make, which is to get ahead of themselves. I constantly reminded myself that it was about making the seat marginal, it wasn't about winning. But no-one who wants to bring about change can afford to operate with just the pilot light on. This was driven home to me most forcefully at a forum in Wodonga, which was attended by the candidates, during the campaign. When it was over and people were milling about, a man called Tom, who I didn't know, came up to me and said, 'You don't really want to win do you?' I looked at him and laughed, and said, 'How do you know that?', and he replied, 'Oh, it's really obvious'. Trying to make light of it, I said, 'That's not good'. He fixed me with a stern look and a tinge of disappointment and responded, 'Well, if you don't want to win, that's fine. But you should say that. You can't pretend.' I realised then that I was in danger of letting down everyone who was working so hard on behalf of our group, if I wasn't in it to win.

At that stage what he was saying was true. Tom had seen right through me and, if he could do that, how many others could do the same? If the only thought you have is that you're going to lose, you will lose. I went home and reflected hard on this. I changed my attitude and said to myself for the remainder of the campaign, 'Okay, we are going to win this. I'm going to do everything in my power to win.' I carried that mantra in my head continuously and did all I could to believe it.

I made the decision that, for the next four months, campaigning would be my occupation, and every day offered a steep learning curve. Initially there was no campaign strategy. Tim Fischer had already given me some guidance, so now it was the turn of Judy Brewer to be consulted. Judy had run in the state seat of Benambra for the National Party when she was in her 20s, and knew what she was talking about. I met with her fortnightly and she tutored me on how to lay out and pursue a campaign strategy. Early on, she told me I should have a numerical target of new people to meet each week and I should aim high. As the campaign progressed, she set a weekly target of 1,000, which turned out not to be too daunting, actually: I just had to go to places where there were people in large numbers. I didn't do a lot of doorknocking, because that wouldn't get me 1,000 people. But setting up a stall on a Saturday morning outside a Coles or at a market would boost my weekly tally. Judy taught me how to focus on community meetings and events which attracted larger numbers of constituents. As the organisational structure grew, with six campaign hubs in larger towns, which we used as jumping-off points for other parts of the electorate, and growing numbers of volunteers, I could easily hit the target if there were, say, five community events.

I soon learnt that I had to be able to explain, succinctly, my role as an independent candidate and future MP, especially in a safe conservative seat. Being an independent was a sensitive matter in 2013. The Gillard government had failed to win a lower house majority at the 2010 election and was thus reliant on crossbench support to hold on to office. The most prominent – and controversial – crossbench supporters were two rural independents from New South Wales, Tony Windsor and Rob Oakeshott. Both had backgrounds in the National Party. Tony had failed to secure National Party preselection for a state seat, which he went on to win as an independent, before taking the federal seat of New England, again as an independent. Rob had been a NSW state MP for the Nationals before leaving the party and then winning the federal seat of Lyne as an independent. When both not only supported a minority Labor government but did so in order to implement a pricing scheme on carbon emissions, there was much talk of betrayal of the traditional conservative values in their seats.

It would be easy for the Liberals to try to cast me as an independent in the Windsor–Oakeshott mould. I had to take every opportunity to emphasise that I would not switch over to backing a Labor government if I had the balance of power – an extremely unlikely prospect anyway, given how badly Labor was trailing in the polls. Even so, I was still bound to be asked as a sort of litmus test question what my position would be if the parliamentary numbers were tight. Fortunately, Tony Windsor helped me out on this. At a very early stage, some of our volunteers had travelled to Canberra to speak with him, looking for campaigning and positioning tips. He shared the line that he had used, which was, 'As an independent I'll support the government of the day', which somehow seemed to defuse the situation, so that became one of my mantras in 2013.

This was not the only assistance Tony gave me. When our Voices for Indi campaign people had talked to him, he offered to support us. This led to an extensive discussion in the campaign team about how to respond. There did not appear to be much upside in getting him directly involved in our campaign, given how much criticism he had faced from the media and from people in his own seat over his support for a minority Labor government. But he found another way to help us.

In late June, more than two months out from election day, he announced that he would not be running again. On the following Sunday, Tony was interviewed via video by Barrie Cassidy on the ABC's *Insiders* program. Rob Oakeshott, who was also retiring, was part of the video hook-up too. Tony and Rob had both won their seats from the National Party. Winding up the interview, Barrie asked Tony, 'As you leave Canberra, who will you miss the least, Tony Windsor?' Tony smiled, and seemed to have his answer ready, although I suspect he hadn't been quite sure he would go ahead with what he wanted to say until that moment. He replied, after a short pause, 'Ah, I've got to say it: Sophie Mirabella. She wins the nasty prize. Now that I might have a bit of time on my hands, I know there's an excellent independent running down there. I might even go down and give them a hand. They've got a great group of people, so the people of Indi, just have a look at your representative and see how much better you could do.' Rob, asked by Barrie if he wanted to add to the list, was amused by Tony's answer and said, 'I'm a lover not a fighter now, but in the interests of unity, I'll agree'.

This national endorsement took my candidacy to another level. It got huge media coverage. The timing was terrific. We were in campaign mode. *The Border Mail* gave Tony's comments about the Indi contest and our local MP a great run the next day, which really helped, because it took what he said far beyond the ABC *Insiders* audience. It also got play in *The Australian*, taking my campaign from local 'also ran' status to something of national significance.

The campaign was ramping up and all around the electorate we asked our supporters to organise events that would give me the opportunity to meet people. The most popular events were Farm Open Days. Colleagues in my Women in Agriculture networks opened their homes and gardens to the community and charged an entry fee. There would be cakes and vegetables and seedlings and pot plants and various other things for sale. I would show up and speak and then invite people to donate to our campaign if they wanted to. We had a lot of these community-based, locally sponsored events, with generally 30–40 people coming along to each one. If you think about who you know and then pick up the phone, you can make a lot of things happen. I would ring a friend or colleague and ask them if they would host an event and they would more often than not agree, 'Oh yes of course I'll do that'. From there, we'd agree on a date. They would then put out an email and invite their friends. That was basically how it worked – the circles pushing out to make bigger circles.

Sometimes, Voices for Indi would put out flyers, depending on the organisational skill of the host, but mostly it was word of mouth, as in 'Come to my place – Cathy's coming, come and meet her and catch up with everyone else'. We did have good social media coverage of these events but mostly it was on the rural grapevine. These events built up local knowledge of what we were doing and it raised money in pretty decent amounts. We would often get $1,000 out of an event and it had the desired bonus for me of keeping me in touch with what was going on in all those communities. Phil Haines, who was the formal campaign director, hosted a garden party that raised $5,000. The enthusiasm kept building and so did the donations.

In Indi, the biggest urban centre of Wodonga was traditionally Liberal-voting. I hoped that the key to winning Wodonga was to activate the community networks. Wodonga is also the closest city to my home in the Indigo Valley. Many of my family and friends are Wodonga-based and that made the political challenge there seem not so insurmountable; it was more about getting out doorknocking and using every network we had to get everybody who knew me or knew my sister who was a doctor, or knew my sister who was a lawyer, or knew my sister and her husband who were dentists in Wodonga. I was the chair of the Catholic Education Board, so I hoped the Catholic vote would be strong. Many of my nieces and nephews had gone to school in Wodonga, and my cousins worked at the hospital. Disaffected Liberals were happy to vote for me because they could see that, if the seat became marginal, that would benefit Wodonga. We had a strong team of volunteers who doorknocked and handed out how-to-vote cards during pre-polling and on election day – well-known stock and station agents, real estate agents, business people with big networks of their own. A little extra for us was that Sophie Mirabella had based herself in Wangaratta, a smaller centre than Wodonga, and had not built up strong community networks of her own in Wodonga. Also Wangaratta was where many of the Voices for Indi people lived. Phil Haines had been president of Wangaratta High School council, I'd taught at Galen College, Helen Haines worked at the hospital. We were the ones with good connections to the institutions in Wangaratta. But we all knew that it takes more than a few good ideas and some solid community connections to get where we wanted to go.

Chapter 7

THE CAMPAIGN

By the time our first campaign was up and running, Voices for Indi had already gone through a series of growth stages in a short time, not unlike a stop-motion film of a flower that bursts through the soil and starts to bloom within a few seconds. Having consulted widely, it was clear that the best and most effective way of having our local voices heard and respected, and our issues acted on in Canberra, was to run an election campaign to frighten the Coalition parties enough to notice us.

This was a massive undertaking and in the next few pages I will go through some of the logistical and strategic steps we had to take just to reach a stage where we were functional. This is the only way to understand fully how we managed to win the seat.

In our first year, there was ongoing tension within Voices for Indi between those who wanted to give priority to spending time and resources on a process for finding and using our voices and those who were inclined to launch a more conventional election campaign. The sweet spot we landed on was to establish the hubs, which satisfied both tendencies. They welded conventional campaigning strategies with community-based grassroots organisational strategies.

It is hard to overstate the importance of the hubs to our campaign. Just about everything we did ran through them. Mostly shopfronts on main streets, the hubs were beacons of hope, and centres of activity.

Orange everywhere: flags blowing in the breeze, corflutes and banners announcing our purpose and calling 'Put Indi First'. Inside the hubs there was warmth, company, food and jobs for volunteers. Jobs for everyone. Butchers paper lined the walls with rosters, timetables, maps, agendas, lists of actions, names, contacts and inspirational sayings. Out the back the kitchens hummed, pumpkin soup a favourite, bowls of fruit and snacks; in a side room the Indi Makers with their sewing machines produced more flags, bunting, jewellery, banners, dog coats and all manner of merchandise.

The hubs were where the training took place under the direction of each hub coordinator: use of social media, preferences, writing letters to newspapers, rules at polling places, role-play in handing out how-to-vote cards and making the case for voting for me, my policies, and how to go doorknocking. They were where the logistics of distributing our bunting, T-shirts and signs were looked after, as well as coordinating and organising local events and forums.

The hubs delivered support to the 600 volunteers we had that first campaign, provided a visual presence in main towns, built community trust, and were places where constituents could seek information and join us. They were pivotal in building the community movement and provided constant feedback to the campaign committee. They were open most weekdays and Saturday in the two months leading up to election day.

We ran a decentralised campaign, which was fitting for the geographically diverse electorate. Our campaign committee based in Wangaratta did the bigger-picture, electorate-wide planning relating to media, advertising and marketing design, the budget, purchasing and coordinating, and our teams and hub leaders were entrusted with independent decision-making. The campaign committee was

THE CAMPAIGN

not some small cabal. It began with 12 members and by the time of the election more than 20 people would attend its meetings. The size and geographical spread of Indi presented a big challenge to our campaign, which we overcame. There were 96 polling places across the electorate and one of our biggest achievements was ensuring that we had teams outside every booth on election day, plus full teams looking after pre-poll voting in Wangaratta, Wodonga and Benalla for the two weeks before September 7. Each polling place had a captain, job descriptions, a roster, and a box of merchandise. After I was elected, the hubs continued to be really important connectors for me. When I needed to find out something in Mansfield, for example, I would email the hub coordinators and ask them to get in touch with their group. They would come back to me quickly with a quality response.

It would be impossible for me to adequately acknowledge or thank the campaign volunteers for their dedication and commitment. Without a doubt it was the volunteers who made the campaigns a success: wearing their orange T-shirts, scarves, warm coats and beanies and waving orange banners and flags, they gave the campaign its sense of all-encompassing colour and movement and made a statement that was impossible to ignore. Thank you for turning up, speaking up and standing up for Indi!

The less tangible side of campaigning, making sure that we kept ourselves true to our values, was a constant challenge. Even though we were running to give the sitting member a fright at the very least, we couldn't afford to descend into criticism, nor could we invite voters to attack the incumbent. Our message was 'If Cathy gets elected she's not going to get caught up in the bickering of politics, it's going to be about community engagement', and so we coined this phrase: 'Being our best selves'.

Everybody who has been involved in community organisations knows the importance of staying focused and managing risk. We required all of our volunteers to sign an agreement. It also had a practical purpose. In order to cover our volunteers with insurance, we needed to get their formal agreement and that also meant agreeing to the campaign values. Once they signed, we put their name in a database and linked them to insurance cover. The agreement read in part, 'The agreement is intended to indicate the respect with which we treat our volunteers. The intention of the agreement is to assure you both of our appreciation of your services and to indicate our commitment to do the very best we can in the volunteer experience.'

During our training sessions at the hubs, we workshopped responses for the volunteers. We posed the question: 'Okay, you're going out doorknocking and someone wants to tell you how bad the current Member of Parliament is. What will you do when that happens?' The agreed response was along the lines of 'We have signed up to the Voices for Indi value statements and we are going to be our best selves, and we totally understand that you've got opinions about the current member but if you don't want more of that then you should vote for Cathy'. It was the way not to engage with personal criticism. I took pains never to talk about the sitting member. We strived to keep the focus on me and what I wanted to do. This was where the tension was, because quite a few people wanted to be critical and tell me stories, and it wasn't helpful.

When you're mounting a community-driven political campaign from what is effectively a standing start, one thing you cannot afford to do is to assume that the wonderful people who step forward to do the work have a great understanding of how to do it. Those of us on the Voices for Indi committee had a decent idea of what we needed to include in our volunteer training but less of a working notion of how to train people. Just like the volunteers, we were learning. We did research about political training techniques and drew on some American examples. Members of Voices for Indi moved around each of the hubs and began the train-the-trainer sessions with some of the high-level material where you have a word or acronym to explain the principles of campaigning. It was good and quite interesting and, when we sought feedback from the hub coordinators, they said, 'Look, it's all important, but the thing we really want to know is: how do we doorknock? Our people are really scared about going out doorknocking. Could we do some training about doorknocking?' It can pay to keep things simple.

In keeping with our rejection of politics-as-usual, we were running an open ticket and weren't directing preferences. We did no deals with any party. We worked on the assumption that voters, after voting number one for me, knew their intentions as to who to put next. Also I hoped that for those who gave me their first vote, that vote would stay with me and not be distributed.

It was important for our volunteers outside the polling places to know exactly how to deliver the cards to voters on their way in. During the training we talked about catching the eye of each voter, asking them if they were interested in one of Cathy's how to vote cards, and if the answer was yes, advising the voter to put a number in every square but make sure that '1' was next to Cathy. We also were strategic about where we placed volunteers outside the polling places. Generally, we positioned two volunteers at each entry point. We put our extroverts on the outer wing and our introverts on the inner wing. For preference training, which we originally approached as just a useful exercise in education about the way the electoral system works, one of our key hub volunteers, a maths teacher, devised an experiential game showing how the votes and preferences flowed based on colours. It turned out to be incredibly popular and that extra understanding among our frontline volunteers about the importance of preferences came in very, very handy on election day. During that first election, we didn't offer scrutineering training because, well, why would we need it? We were in for a surprise.

Even if we were not running an ordinary campaign, the traditional marketing, branding and merchandise of campaigns was not something we could afford to ignore. Indeed, we did it but in an Indi, country community way. We had the Indi Makers, artists and tradespeople who produced hand-made merchandise, badges, jewellery, flags, bunting, orange-painted chairs, screen-printed banners and table cloths for polling tables. We ran street stalls and fundraisers, held street walks and constituent forums, and had groups of singers walking through shopping centres singing our theme song, an adaption with permission of 'From Little Things Big Things Grow', before many of our major events. We sought endorsements from high-profile locals, such as footballers and leading farmers, and asked them to place 'Vote 1 Cathy' signs on their front gates. This had a big impact in the rural parts of Indi.

And we had enthusiastic campaign teams. There was a media team that covered traditional media and social media depending on the skills of each team member. We had a finance team looking after our budget and a legal team ensuring that we adhered to the electoral rules, kept our messaging within the law and managed risk assessment. All this was put together inside four months, with no pre-existing infrastructure.

It was vital that I presented as serious, professional and ready to take on the responsibility of representing the people of Indi. To this end, I established a constituent enquiry team, which enabled me to show voters how I would respond to them as an MP. From my time with Mr Cameron, I knew how to do this. Two amazing women volunteered to do the constituent work in the Wodonga office. When volunteers were doorknocking and a voter told us about an issue that concerned them, the volunteers would come back to the office and give the details to the constituent staff who would write a formal letter to that voter as if I was an MP. It would go along the lines of 'Dear so and so, our doorknocking team has told me that you've got such and such a problem. This is a really important issue. I'll make sure that if I get elected I will attend to this straight away, but in the meantime here are three things you can do' – then I'd list those steps and finish 'Yours sincerely, Cathy McGowan, Independent Candidate for Indi'. From June until election day, the team did that work full-time, which built up my image as the local MP-in-waiting.

As a result of the kitchen table conversations and the Indi report, we began our campaign armed with deep knowledge of what our fellow constituents thought about the northeast and what they wanted. They loved the place and wanted values-based representation, with a focus on respect and integrity. They were not hung up on policy; for them, services had a higher priority. They wanted to be consulted and involved, and they wanted something better. Many were prepared to step up to secure what they wanted, but they needed leadership and to be shown how to get the change they wanted.

Our job was to connect them with the belief that if they supported me they could get closer to making that change happen. We workshopped how we could do this and, boiled down, the message was that they had nothing to lose and everything to gain by backing me, because things needed to change, the Liberals were going to win the election and this was the way to get them to take notice of us. Voting for me was one way to step up. Another was to call in to a hub and volunteer or to talk to their family, friends, neighbours and work colleagues. We were aiming for one-quarter of the primary votes in the seat. We needed preferences from National Party, Labor and Greens voters. Could we get disaffected Liberals and Nationals to give us their primary vote? That's what we were looking for. Young people were targeted with an appeal to their idealism and the need for action on climate change, transport, telecommunication, mental health and my support for action on marriage equality.

The politics of our entry into the race worked in several ways. There was the 'What is an independent?' question; there was the differentiation from the sitting member, or more specifically, the difference between her way of being the member and what I said my way would be. There was the challenge of finding out how we could attract the dormant National Party vote in the seat – that is, the natural National Party voters who voted Liberal because the Coalition rules prohibited their party running a candidate while there was a Liberal incumbent. Among National Party members with whom I came into contact, there was often a subtly delivered sense of friendly permission granted to me. They all knew, especially the older farmers who'd seen a lot, that if an independent won, under the rules that would give the National Party a chance to run a candidate against the Liberals at the next election. They were confident that if they ran a National Party candidate, they would win the seat, although subsequent elections would prove that assumption wrong. The enthusiastic endorsement from Ken Jasper, 34 years a National Party MP in the Victorian Parliament, helped me enormously on this front.

Adjacent to this was a broader question: how would we convince this conservative community to vote for an independent? In speeches,

THE CAMPAIGN

I explored a range of reasons. They varied from the very pragmatic 'I'm a local and you can trust me', to 'Independents get things done and nothing's happened here for a long time, and we want to get things done', to 'You've got a choice about how you want your community to be; we're giving you a choice. And do you want more of the same or something different?' Variations on a theme, I suppose. I also was more explicit about my role as a community representative: 'Voices for Indi are offering something different. The way we're doing it, through community participation, is the way we're going to do politics, so we're giving you that choice.' We were upfront about that choice and it worked for us in terms of managing and extending our message into the electorate.

We kept ourselves removed from the orthodox Labor–Liberal–Green debates. That was one of our points of difference from the major parties. Increasingly, we had many people visiting the hubs and at our events and community meetings telling us that they believed they could have something better. We could see that it was working. There was a 'What have we got to lose?' feeling for some people. Keeping ourselves out of the nitty gritty of the traditional bickering was a huge strength. When we were asked about other people in politics, along the lines of 'How would you work with Tony Abbott?', I would say, 'Tony will come and see me. We'll talk. Let's move on.' People liked this approach, which indicated that I wasn't going to get bogged down in acting like I was some sort of national kingmaker: I would concentrate on representing the people of Indi.

Our volunteer campaign workers urged voters to give me their second preference if they couldn't bring themselves to put a '1' next to my name on the ballot paper. We were after every preference we could get. We encouraged our volunteers to look for where they could get that one extra vote. The intensity built up as we got closer to the election.

We were putting our beliefs into action. The problem we were trying to overcome was sharply defined. The circumstances felt right. We had the correct timeframe, the motivation and a practical purpose to mobilise the community. The problem was a lack of recognition of our voice. The solution was to establish a process for engaging so that a diversity of voices could be raised in Canberra. The community came on board and agreed to engage and participate. It wanted its multiplicity of voices to be heard and acted on. Using these voices in an election campaign was the most practical and immediate way of doing this. Voices for Indi was a committee, a small organisation that created a movement built on structures, values and behaviour.

We campaigned so strongly that by August the Liberal Party realised we were around in a serious way. They boosted their investment in their campaign, bringing Tony Abbott to Wodonga and making robo-calls to voters. To my team this was a good sign, especially since they were following the standard big-party electioneering template, which was such a contrast from what we were doing. Everything they did was built on the assumption that the people who decide elections don't pay attention until that hot period between the moment the pre-poll voting begins and election day. We had been running a different, cool-burn campaign over a much longer timeframe, built on hope, belief in the wisdom and energies of locals, and the desire for something better.

Chapter 8

INDI TURNS ORANGE

And then the thing that we did not expect to happen, happened: we won. At the close of voting on election night, the result was on a knife-edge. It would take another 11 days before the final pre-poll and postal votes were counted, and I was declared the winner.

We realised we were getting close to our goal of pushing Indi into the marginal zone in those two weeks before the election, when the Liberal Party swung serious resources into the seat. But winning? No. At the previous election, Sophie's vote after preferences had been distributed was 59.19 per cent. To win, we needed to roll back that preferred vote by 8 or 9 per cent to make the contest really tight. Six or 7 per cent would have been good too. That still would have rendered Indi marginal and forced the Liberals to take notice of what our electorate needed. But when translated into people voting, these were big numbers, especially when a swing towards the Liberals was expected across the country because of the collapse of the Labor Party in government. I needed to get those preferences into the equation. The important target for us was to get the Liberal primary vote down below 50 per cent, which would mean that preferences would be counted and hopefully flow my way. I was one of 12 candidates running in this election, so once the outcome was reliant on the preference count, technically, all sorts of things were possible because of the preference flow. And I knew from my research that Andrew Wilkie, in 2010 in Hobart, had come from 3rd position on primary votes, to win on the preference flow. We just had to get Sophie's primary vote below 50 per cent, then those hoped-for National Party, Greens and Labor preferences would kick in.

On election night, once we saw the numbers, we were overjoyed, of course. We had achieved what we set out to achieve: we had frightened the Liberals and from now on they wouldn't be able to ignore us. We had made the seat marginal. We were no longer a safe seat and what Voices for Indi was offering was taken seriously by a lot of our fellow electors. But could we actually get over the line? I still thought it was unlikely. The Liberal postal vote and pre-poll vote operation was well-oiled, whereas we were finding our way.

Because the preference flows did not go in the conventional Liberal–Labor way and instead produced a tight vote count in which only the Liberal or independent could prevail, the Electoral Commission had to conduct a recount. In effect, it had to start the count again. In the days that followed and as the recount got underway, we needed to do everything we could to honour our commitment to the supporters and secure every one of those votes. We got serious. We were in this with a real shot and we needed scrutineers – people with an understanding of the voting laws who could watch the counting of each ballot paper and ensure that only the valid votes were tallied. We weren't prepared for scrutineering and put out a call, collecting our most numerate and politically minded friends from wherever we could get them in the electorate and in Melbourne, Sydney and Canberra. The response was strong and people gathered for the fray, taking days off work, and locally we set up a scrutineering accommodation and food roster and management plan.

On the Monday following the election, as the team gathered in Wangaratta for our first round of scrutineering training, I knew the next few days were critical. I wasn't there for the training – as a candidate, I could not attend the count – and when the opportunity arose to give the scrutineering team a pep talk by phone, I reached deep into my emotional bank account. I encouraged them to find and fight for every single vote because I wanted to make an apology to the members of the Stolen Generation who lived in Indi – an apology from which Sophie Mirabella had excluded herself when the federal parliament gave its apology in 2008. We owed it to the First Nations peoples of this country to make a genuine apology, to work towards reconciliation, truth telling and a treaty.

Years earlier, when I bought my farm, I did not believe I owned the land, I was merely a custodian. Indigenous Australians had held it for thousands of years before white people, including my forebears, made their way to the district. I had been annoyed that my local member had not been part of the apology and I wanted to put that right. I wanted Indi to have another kind of voice in parliament that reflected deeply held values, where community came before party and factional politics. I heard my voice break as I shared this with the team. And as the recounting got underway, there were tensions within the counting place as there was so much at stake. The postal votes were favouring Sophie and every day she clawed back numbers. It was only the discovery of 1,000 misplaced votes on the Monday of the second week after the election that took us over the line. In the final count, with all the preferences counted, I was ahead of Sophie by 439 votes.

The preference allocation split this way: 4,517 votes for Sophie and 16,978 votes for me – I got a shade less than 80 per cent of the preferences. I secured 27,763 primary votes or 31.18 per cent of the total. Sophie's primary vote fell by almost 5,000 to 39,785 votes or 44.68 of the total. This was not good for her. In 2010, her primary vote had been 52.62 per cent. The combined Labor and Greens vote fell by about 17,000 – close to 22 per cent. It's only rough arithmetic, but if you add the Liberals who deserted Sophie to the voters who peeled off the ALP and the Greens, you get close to my primary vote.

We had set out to attain political power by making the seat marginal, but along the way we found a way to accumulate more power than we originally intended. That was a good thing. And our model was never intended to create a political cult around me, or to give me much personal power at all; our aim was to reflect the wishes of the community. Even so, I must have been a little discomfited for a while. When I got to Canberra as the member for Indi the following month, I was interviewed for the National Library. The audio file of the interview is available on the library's website, and listening to it years later I can still hear the emotion in my voice.

Despite that, let me tell you that in the moment of discovering that we had won, the feeling was wonderful. My diary from September 18, when the count concluded, reads 'Malcolm Fraser rang me, absolutely delighted, wants to meet with me. Andrew Broad from Mallee, National Party, rang. Darren Chester, Gippsland rang. Adam Bandt, Greens, rang. All offered their support. Media everywhere wants to know the how and what of it all.' On September 21: 'Well, it's all over bar the formal declaration. Huge party last night in Oxley, 600 orange supporters turned up, a tremendous feeling, absolutely amazing sense of celebration. My voice has gone, hard to talk, particularly hard to talk to the crowd'.

But the next day reality set in: 'Sunday, very tired. The confession: I so don't want to be a politician, really, I don't. Why did I say yes? Because I was asked. Because Leah, Ben, and the young people wanted me to do it, because I thought it could be possible, it could be done.

Someone like me with the skills, network experience, motivation to pull it off. I thought it would be a hard job, but it could be done, and maybe there's a touch of competitiveness, a good chance to show that rural Australia can do this. Okay, it's all happened. Now I'm the MP, how can I turn it around so that I enjoy it? How can I lift the terrible heavy weight on my shoulders? I've lost my life, my lovely life. I've now got a new job.'

But the truth is, I quickly came to love being the member for Indi, though first I had to learn how to do this new job. One serious advantage I had was my past experience as a member of an MP's staff.

I had so much to learn, particularly about how to be an MP, so I started looking for mentors. First cab off the rank was Tim Fischer, who had already been so helpful. When I reached out, he agreed to help me yet again, but he was clear that he wouldn't do anything that would conflict with the direct interests of the National Party. I explained that I wasn't looking for policy advice, I needed to understand how parliament worked and what was required from an MP. He was happy to help me on that basis. Tim and Judy came for afternoon tea soon after, where he gave me a written list of tips and offered other advice that I hurriedly wrote down in a notebook. It's advice I followed to the letter and am pleased to share with all aspiring independent politicians: don't expect ministers to visit the electorate, as the government wouldn't want to do anything that might make me look good. Instead, invite ambassadors to visit Indi, because those visits would suggest I had influence and might generate local media interest. And they did.

Over the years many of the diplomatic corps accepted my invitation to visit Indi to great local publicity and interest. A highlight also was the electoral visit by the Governor-General Sir Peter Cosgrove and his wife Lynn in 2015. Another useful suggestion was to make one country a special place of interest outside your electorate. I had worked in Papua New Guinea during my time as a consultant, and was keen to maintain the connection and subsequently joined the Parliamentary Friends of PNG. As a result of this interest, I formed a productive relationship with Julie Bishop, minister for foreign affairs, and in 2017 I was part of the Australian delegation to PNG to monitor its national elections.

Other advice covered the rules of accountability for public money and the need to avoid being in receipt of any government funding; I had ongoing agricultural contracts from my consultancy days, but as I had already passed those over to my younger partners I was clear in this regard. Tim understood that I needed to build a strong local media profile and he suggested getting climate change experts to visit, and making it my business to know the decision-makers who had influence over the issues I needed to address. He suggested I go to Adelaide during the parliamentary recess to meet the head of the Australian Rail Track Corporation because one of my big issues was getting our train line fixed.

Another piece of delicate advice about constituents, some of whom he referred to as 'time wasters', was that I should get my staff to ask constituents to prepare a summary of issues, no more than two pages which outlined challenges and solutions. It was common for constituents to complain about an issue and I found that, once I asked them to put it in writing, their issue would often fizzle away and you wouldn't hear from them on that topic again. But if it was serious enough for them to put it in writing, they'd already done the thinking and it would take both of us closer to doing something meaningful. He was emphatic about the need to reply to all correspondence. Failure to do so was deadly.

Tim also pointed out that any Member of Parliament had the right to request a minister to provide a departmental briefing on any topic, and particularly legislation before the parliament. I took early advantage of this advice and my first request was to environment minister Greg Hunt for a briefing on the Abbott government's controversial carbon trading scheme and its policy on emission buy-backs. The Labor Party's so-called carbon tax was a central national issue during the campaign and I had committed not to support its repeal. Finally, he warned me not to sit at the wrong table in the members' dining room at Parliament House, where the parties sat at separate tables. Who knew? I mostly kept away from the dining room in my first term unless I had guests.

Tim died in 2019, aged 73. He wasn't crazy about independents, but he was generous to me.

Chapter 9

USING THE COURAGE MUSCLE

My first day in parliament was one of mixed emotions. It had been a long and exciting journey, shared with so many wonderful people along the way, not the least of who were the members of my family. It was with great pride that I stood at the dispatch table, looked up into the gallery and saw them all gathered to witness my pledge, and, with a Bible given to me by the staff and students from Galen College, took the oath and signed the pledge. Ever loyal to me, many of my family gathered again in Canberra for the next major event, my first speech. On December 2, just three days after my 60th birthday, the gallery was full to bursting with hundreds of orange-clad family, friends and busloads of Indi residents who had paid their own way and made the trip north to witness my 'maiden' speech and to be part of history – celebrating Indi's first independent and Australia's first female independent MP. We had a wonderful day.

At the induction day for new MPs, the Speaker in the previous parliament, Anna Burke, told us about the Federation Chamber, a smaller parallel mini-parliamentary chamber where members could speak about constituency matters, make 90-second statements and generally not be noticed. I thought I could spend a lot of time there and then disappear at the next election. When I shared this view with my circle of trusted advisors, they were shocked and said, 'Why would you do that? You'd only be a one-term wonder, the Liberals would get the seat back and all the change you've talked about wouldn't have happened.' Of course, they were right. I had to put aside any jitters, embrace being a public figure, put everything into this and do the job well.

I set myself to tackle this job as a six-year, two-term project, just as I would have when working as a consultant, designing it in a way that suited my strengths – and the special characteristics of Voices for Indi. And I was going to like it! Voices for Indi and its ethos simply had to be strong, supporting another independent member after I'd shuffled off. That became the goal.

On that first day I was given a warm welcome by many MPs, which eased my state of mind. On the crossbench, I was seated next to Clive Palmer, who had won the Queensland seat of Fairfax for his Palmer United Party, defeating the Liberal candidate by 53 votes. His party also won three Senate seats. Clive proudly claimed to have put me in parliament because his candidate in Indi gave me his preferences. While I knew Clive's background as a mining magnate, I didn't know much else about him and was open to a friendship, and over the months ahead we formed a most unlikely alliance around some aspects of the government's carbon tax legislation. Interestingly, on the same day, his fellow Queenslander Kevin Rudd, with whom I was more familiar, also sought credit for handing me the seat, claiming that he had personally ensured that Indi's Labor voters gave me their preference votes.

Clive told me that Tony Abbott, our new Prime Minister, was only interested in politics and had no interest in policy. It was a useful reflection. I met Tony later in the day outside the House and we shook hands. He said he was disappointed that I'd won but congratulated me.

Labor's Jenny Macklin, whose father had been the shire engineer at Wangaratta, offered to help and support me, as did Tanya Plibersek, Kate Ellis and Catherine King. Jane Prentice, a Liberal MP from Queensland, also had connections to Wangaratta and offered her help and support. Jane and I shared a love of PNG and we were both active in the Parliamentary Friends of PNG group. Anthony Albanese advised me to camp outside the office of Warren Truss, the Minister for Infrastructure and Regional Development, until I got a meeting. National Party MPs Barnaby Joyce and John Cobb came up and said hello.

The overwhelming sense of that first day was of a huge welcome, people across the political spectrum were pleased to see me there. I was surprised but I also concluded that if you ever had to become an independent MP, the way to do it was to win the way we had done, which was legitimately from a community base. They could see that we'd won because we'd had a good strategy that introduced real competition in the system, and that I'd won fairly.

That was all gratifying but I still had to overcome a big hurdle, which was that although I'd worked out through trial and error how to become a successful candidate, I didn't know yet how to be an effective parliamentarian or a politician. The best way to solve a problem like that is to ask for advice, so that's what I did. Tim Fischer's guidance had been valuable – and I would look to him for help again in the future – but this time I turned to two other National Party politicians. Peter Walsh has been a National Party MP in the Victorian Parliament since 2002 and became party leader in 2014. We had met years earlier on the Australian Rural Leadership Program. I asked him for any advice he could give, and he was good enough to meet me in Melbourne and speak by phone after that. He was incredibly helpful, explaining the practicalities of constituent letters, setting up routines in the office, and how to manage my time, which would be divided between parliamentary sitting weeks and constituent work in the electorate. He said it was vital to have a strategy, because the job was just so big you could spend all your time merely reacting to things.

Peter gave me clever, practical office management advice for a big rural electorate. His practice was to set up big wall-charts with your communities across the bottom and issues along the side, and make sure that there was a balance of time shared between electorate communities and interest groups. Throughout an electoral term it was important to have covered personal meetings so that everybody was looked after. The local state MP for Murray Valley, based in Wangaratta, Tim McCurdy, was another Australian Rural Leadership Program alumnus. Tim warned me the job by its very nature was reactive, with people coming in the door all the time and political things happening that were outside your control. 'Unless you decide what you want to do and carve out time to devote to it, you're in danger of going under as wave after wave of events and demands consume you.'

And this time I turned to Tony Windsor for help. Having retired from parliament, he visited Canberra from time to time and we caught up. He put me in touch with his former advisor John Clements. John seemed to have a deep understanding of how everything functioned, especially in the agricultural policy area. I needed a political advisor and I asked him if he'd take the job, but he wasn't interested. Instead, he offered to mentor me, giving me help when I needed it. In our first good discussion, he advised me to get to know the senators. This made sense because the incoming Senate elected at the 2013 election had a massive crossbench, with the Abbott government needing six extra votes to pass legislation. That was where the legislative pressure points were. In those early months, I set out a timetable so that I could meet every Victorian senator and made it my business to know them and their interests. After that I moved on to senators from the other states, concentrating on the ones from the crossbench and the regions. This was a comfortable space in which to work. It was community work 101: build your networks.

Personally, I quickly got into a surprisingly familiar groove. Many generous friends offered me accommodation in Canberra, and it was with pleasure that I reconnected with an old friend with whom I had shared a house in my days working with Mr Cameron in Old Parliament House. Even my old room was available and we slipped into the same arrangement we'd had 30 years earlier. She was now a senior public servant and her duplex by Lake Burley Griffin would be my refuge. It was a struggle leaving home on the Sunday afternoon of a sitting week, saying goodbye to my home and farm, attending to the chores, organising the sheep with fresh feed and water, checking the garden, picking flowers for the office, and packing four jackets, four tops, two sets of blue and black slacks, four pairs of shoes (blue and black) and heading off in my car on the four-hour trip. On the way, I would use the time to make calls to constituents, family and friends and plan the week's work.

Just on my politician's wardrobe: I have always appreciated the importance of first impressions and appearance as critical elements of being in the public eye, but, during the campaign and once in Parliament, clothes and wardrobe assumed an even higher relevance and it took me a while to find my style. Eventually I settled on two wardrobes: one for Canberra loosely styled on Hilary Clinton's pants suits and a more complex one for the electorate. The latter required extra flexibility in order to cover a day in the office, a street walk, a community event, evening functions and a likely media press conference thrown in for good measure. My tips: beware of clashing colours and patterns, keep jewellery to a minimum, wear comfortable shoes and always use makeup.

Some politicians talk of feeling alone in Parliament House, but I never felt that way. I loved the grandeur and beauty of the building and every day took time to enjoy the gardens and views. The location of my office also contributed to this feeling of inclusiveness. My immediate neighbours were Adam Bandt and Clive Palmer. While we may have had political differences, as in most communities our interdependence and need for each other was greater than our differences. Shortly after my election in 2013, Adam phoned to congratulate me and offered his help and advice. I was pleased to accept and made an early trip to Melbourne to meet him and his staff and talk through the practical aspects of running the office, working with volunteers, handling constituent issues and correspondence.

One position Adam and I shared was the need for action to tackle climate change. The Abbott government's repeal of the carbon tax – officially known as the Clean Energy Legislation (Carbon Tax Repeal) Bill 2014 – was one of the early pieces of legislation that required my vote. Initially introduced by Julia Gillard, the energy reform package was called the Clean Energy Futures Plan. In repealing this legislation the government introduced a package of eight bills that would also do away with the architecture linked to action on climate change, specifically the Clean Energy Finance Corporation (CEFC), Climate Change Authority (CCA) and the Australian Renewable Energy Agency (ARENA), all of which the Abbott government wanted to abolish. The need for positive and strong action on climate change was raised during the kitchen table conversations and was a key plank in my policy platform. I was committed to supporting Gillard's legislation, which meant opposing the government's plan to repeal it and it was with a tinge of pride, perhaps even satisfaction, that I sat with the Labor opposition and members of the crossbench – Adam Bandt and Andrew Wilkie – to vote 'no' on behalf of my electorate. This is what I had been elected to do: to take Indi's voice to parliament and vote on matters of principle.

An interesting aspect of this package of legislation was the role played by Clive and the three Palmer United Party Senators in preserving the CEFC, CCA and ARENA. I had a small part to play in these discussions. As I came to know Clive, I discovered we had much in common, including a strong love for regional Australia, and an interest in global politics and innovation. Clive's office was a few doors from mine, and, with our respective staff, we developed a working relationship based on mutual respect and understanding. During the long evenings it wasn't unusual for us to check in on each other and our staff, talk about the day, share information on legislation coming before the parliament, discuss how we would vote and, from time to time, agree to disagree.

Consequently, I was delighted to be invited by Clive to a private dinner in Parliament House to meet and sit next to former American vice-president and strong environmentalist, Al Gore. We talked about the future of the planet, the importance of community activism and engagement around climate change – clearly topics dear to my heart – and the critical role of politics. I was delighted when Clive announced following that dinner that the Palmer United Party would not be supporting the abolition of the CEFC and ARENA in the Senate, and without those critical votes that part of the legislation failed. In later years I was to work closely with both these organisations and was thrilled when ARENA decided to invest in community-based renewable energy projects in Indi.

The parliamentary agenda was full, the days were long, beginning no later than 8am and finishing at 10pm, and it was a huge job to be across every piece of legislation – and we tried. However, there was one occasion when I slipped up. Early in the piece I voted with the government on a social security bill that I didn't really understand and Jenny Macklin came up to me afterwards and asked, 'Why did you vote with the government on that, Cathy? You couldn't possibly support it.' It turned out that the legislation was about something totally different to what I had thought it was about. Perhaps my vote wouldn't have made a difference, given the size of the government's majority in the House of Representatives, but my number one rule was to always vote for the best outcomes for Indi.

I felt incredibly distressed by this episode, so I rang one of my trusted advisors later in the evening and asked for advice about undoing my vote. I learnt that it was possible to repeal a vote, but it would be unwise because it would draw attention to the fact that I'd got it wrong. Slowly as I let go of my panic I realised the Liberal Party in Indi would definitely notice that I'd reversed a vote and use it against me, whereas they wouldn't hold anything against me for voting with the government, so why not put it down to experience? It was good advice.

I did let it go and I knew here was another big knowledge gap I had to fill, and quickly. I had to get up to speed on the details of how the parliament actually worked, understand the procedures and practices. It led me to develop important professional relationships that, combined

USING THE COURAGE MUSCLE

with John Clements' advice about getting to know the senators, helped me on my journey to become an effective member for Indi.

Another unlikely close professional relationship from those years was with Christopher Pyne. Christopher was the Leader of the House – the one who managed the government's business in the House of Representatives. He was also education minister, an area of special interest for me and one that was so important for my electorate. I knew Christopher came from South Australia and I also knew that we needed to have a positive working relationship. I was now on a big learning curve not just to familiarise myself with Christopher but to get to know all the other members of the House, especially the ministers and the key backbenchers.

This was not an insurmountable challenge; I read up on Christopher, about his background and his electorate, and read his first speech. I studied him. And then I crammed on the other MPs. I went to the parliamentary library and printed out an electoral map of Australia and put it up on a wall and put a list of all the MPs in alphabetical order in our office kitchen, so that everyone in the office could also see who was who and where they came from. I also printed out photos and first speeches of all of the MPs and put them in a folder. In that first year in parliament, I familiarised myself with everybody. And when they made speeches or asked questions I'd be thinking, 'Oh, that's so and so, and that's where they're from'. It took me a long time to memorise because so many of them look alike, especially on the government's side – mostly blokes, dressed the same, speaking the same, sounding the same.

It would be true to say that in all of my time in parliament I carried the responsibility of being a representative of my electorate very heavily – I knew that for just under half of the electorate I was not their first preference, and I wanted to make sure I represented their interests. Combined with this responsibility was a low level of stress and fear of stuff-ups – I often felt that I was only one minute, one question, one slip-up away from public humiliation. I was also conscious in that first year that Sophie, who I knew was very unhappy about being defeated, was watching every single thing I did. And there were regular letters to the editor in the local press and comments on social media that were critical of me – that I was a dud and that people had made the wrong choice. But I chose to harness that fear into something useful, so I studied. I've always been interested in systems and how they work – it was an important part of my postgraduate study – so I found reading about parliamentary practice and rules as close to enjoyable as you could expect.

At the same time, I blended my community-building practices to my enthusiasm for systems. Looking beyond the MPs, I wondered if I could apply systems thinking to the whole building and all the people who worked in it. Parliament House is a system, so I mapped it and worked my way through to understanding it. That proved to be such a useful tool. I liken Parliament House to a game between two AFL football teams. There are the players, who everyone concentrates on. But set them aside. They actually rely on a system that includes umpires and volunteers and support staff, all working together to create a contest. The players are what you are looking at but what you're watching is the sum total of the efforts of many more people who aren't on the ground.

I was curious about the over 5,000 people who worked in Parliament House and then set about getting to know them – the librarians, the committee staff, clerks, guides, Hansard reporters, security guards, the cafe people, the hairdressers, the gardeners, the mail delivery people.

And not only getting to know them but to develop relationships and find out what they knew about what was going on each day. Over time these relationships paid real dividends. The attendants who dropped off mail to our office would begin with 'Hi Cathy. Good morning!' and then bring me up to speed with a small piece of relevant information about the running of the building.

Over time, my staff and volunteers created a small community centred around my parliamentary office. It reminded me in many ways of the atmosphere during the campaign in the hubs. The office was a busy place, people were always coming and going, deputations, visitors, volunteers, staff from other offices, and the phones constantly ringing. We had our fair share of butchers paper on the wall listing jobs, agendas, commitments, and importantly my voting decision-making framework – the first consideration being 'Is this right?' The rooms were full of flowers and pot plants, the walls decorated with a large map of Indi, and, thanks to the Indi Makers, beautifully embroidered hangings and quilts. Pride of place was my fine china (needless to say, orange) tea set and it was such a joy to entertain guests with morning or afternoon tea, enjoying homemade cakes and slices. I suspect this ritual of country hospitality, of taking time to appreciate good food and company, played a key role in my mental health and maintaining a positive attitude in what could be stressful circumstances.

My staff developed a practice of what we called 'working Parliament House': when we needed to find information, we would check in with staff from other offices, ask at the hairdresser's if they'd heard anything, check the press gallery and media or the queue at the coffee cart. Our offices became a go-to place for what was going on, certainly in our little section of Parliament House. This was important, because information in Parliament House flows through the parties and not being a member of a party could be a real disadvantage. The parties met every Tuesday morning to share information and smaller specialised strategic groups meet every day to design tactics including Question Time and speaking rosters. I had to find other ways of getting information.

There were fixtures on the political and legislative calendar that as an MP I had to deal with, no matter how unconventional my approach to politics was. My first federal budget was the first Abbott government budget, delivered by Joe Hockey. I'd been the member for Indi for eight months. It was a shocker, with cuts in areas where Tony Abbott had promised there wouldn't be cuts, a $7 Medicare co-payment, changes to unemployment benefits and much more, plus what I thought was a sanctimonious speech by Hockey that sought to divide Australians into 'lifters' and 'leaners'. I was shaken by it and not sure what to do.

When Labor's Bill Shorten gave his budget-in-reply speech later that week, tearing the budget apart, he was convincing. The media were asking me about my position; as a newcomer, an independent and community politician, they were curious about how I would manage this. This was the beginning of a fruitful, respectful relationship with several reporters in the press gallery, who were open to discussing ideas, strategies and alternative positions. On this occasion, in response to their queries I hedged. I wasn't sure. At a late-night session in my office, one of my staff piped up, 'Cathy, you've always said you'll go and ask your community about things, so why don't you ask the Indi community about this?' This was good advice: of course, why not do what I said I'd do?

We decided to run a community survey and that became our practice with every subsequent budget. It was a simple survey: what did they like and not like about the budget, and was there anything else they wanted to say? We started with our Voices for Indi campaign volunteers, then expanded across the electorate, visiting all the major towns as well as going online. Compiling the feedback for the report was an enormous job for the staff and we ended up asking a volunteer team to come into the office to help with the data entry. And I spent every moment of the working day outside post offices, supermarkets and shopping centres or standing at the entrance to the Wangaratta football oval wearing my orange Voices for Indi T-shirt talking to everybody and asking them to fill in our survey. And we took the orange caravan with us everywhere.

We ended up with high-quality data and analysis which we compiled into the inaugural Indi budget report. I sent a copy of that report to every minister and opposition frontbencher and widely through the electorate. The community loved it and it got excellent local media coverage. It also meant that when I came to do my budget speech, I knew what my community wanted, and I was not working from some assumption about what the people of Indi thought. I ended up voting with the government, because that's what people said they wanted me to do. They also wanted me to make sure I told Abbott and Hockey, and whoever else wanted to hear, about the parts of it that they didn't like. I didn't need to be as concerned about my vote, given that the Labor opposition traditionally supports the budget on the floor of the House. When the vote took place only Clive Palmer and Andrew Wilkie voted against it.

By mid-2014, I had found my voice and was growing in confidence when Christopher Pyne introduced the Higher Education and Research Bill. It was essentially designed to privatise Australia's universities. When I read the bill, I knew immediately what it would mean for Indi – devastation for non-metropolitan universities. If it went through, it would mean that in Victoria the universities of Melbourne and Monash would get even bigger and the regional universities would be left behind, unable to compete.

I contacted the Vice-Chancellor of La Trobe University which has for many years had a Wodonga campus (in fact I had taught there previously), and Charles Sturt University over the border in Albury, and asked how we could work together. Understandably and correctly, they regarded it as terrible policy for their universities. La Trobe took the lead and organised a community forum in Wodonga in February 2015. Charles Sturt University and the Regional Universities Network attended, as did representatives from the Greens and Labor. The outcome was a joint statement calling for a higher education policy that actively supported the regions and clear direction for me to oppose the legislation.

When we returned to parliament, I asked some of the National Party MPs about their position. Privately, I thought they might vote against the legislation because it would have such a negative impact on their electorates. One MP, with a university campus in his electorate, said, 'No, the education portfolio is managed by the Liberals; we don't manage that'. I heard the words, but I couldn't process what he was saying. Was this what being part of the Liberal–National Coalition meant: voting against the best interests of your own constituents? He was telling me that they didn't interfere with portfolio management. I was incredulous and replied, 'But this is going to have a huge impact'.

He advised me to talk with Bridget McKenzie, National Party Senator from Victoria, as she was the Nationals' regional education spokesperson. When I spoke to Bridget, she said she might speak up in the party room but she wasn't going to oppose it in the Senate. Further down the track, I ended up doing some good work with Bridget around finance for regional students, and she came to Wangaratta,

USING THE COURAGE MUSCLE

supporting a CSU campus attached to the TAFE college, but she wasn't going to oppose this legislation. I came away from that meeting thinking 'Really? Is mine the only voice for regional universities in the House of Representatives? If I don't speak up, no-one else will. And if this gets through the Senate, that's the end of quality universities in Albury–Wodonga.'

There was so much available information about the vital role of regional universities, not only in teaching, learning and research, but also as a driver of economic change and workforce development. Labor confirmed they were going to vote 'no' as were the Greens, but, combined, Labor and the Greens didn't have a majority in the Senate. This was when the power of the Senate crossbench and getting to know the senators, and the potential role I might be able to play on regional policy, started to dawn on me.

I arranged meetings with the senators. Ricky Muir, from the Motoring Enthusiast Party, lived in Gippsland in regional Victoria; Jacqui Lambie, from the Palmer United Party, was from Devonport in regional Tasmania; John Madigan, from the Democratic Labour Party, also lived in regional Victoria. They weren't impressed.

Even though this was an awful, destructive bit of policy and I wish it had never been proposed, I was lucky in a sense that it came about, because it allowed me to capitalise on one of my early bits of parliamentary study, getting to know Christopher Pyne.

My original interest was in his capacity as the manager of the government's business and now his role as education minister was the key part of this episode. I found him interesting and entertaining. He had a respectful manner and would always engage with me, even though my vote in the lower house did not matter numerically. I suppose in a way that for him it was an investment in the future. Who knew when the government might need my vote to get across the line, perhaps in the next parliament or the one after that if we were all still around? Anyway, when I told him I wouldn't be supporting the bill, he said, 'Well, I want you to vote with me on this, Cathy. You can have access to all my staff, all my briefings', which I appreciated but it didn't change my position.

Resisting the overtures of the government was a confronting experience and my courage muscle got a good workout. Standing up for myself, for my electorate and for the university sector was a challenge. I care passionately about education – it's had such a powerful role in my life. And possibly because I knew Christopher, of all the ministers, I was eventually prepared to take him on. For the first time, I felt I had a deep understanding of an important piece of legislation. I was sure I had done all my homework and that was, perhaps paradoxically, because his staff had given me such comprehensive briefings at Christopher's direction.

The bill was defeated in late 2014 in the Senate, going down by one vote 31–33. Straight away the government re-introduced it into the House of Representatives – a different version but basically the same bill. That got knocked off too, in March 2015, and the numbers there were 30–34. I only played a small part in stopping this policy. It was a result of the teamwork of Labor, the Greens, Clive Palmer and his team, and me, and we'd all worked together to make sure we had the votes in the Senate. For me, it was about learning how to show the government that it couldn't just do whatever it wanted to do, especially when what it wanted to do did not take into account its likely impact on rural and regional Australia. In retrospect, I can see that this exercise was my beginning as a fully functioning Member of Parliament.

USING THE COURAGE MUSCLE

After that experience I got a real sense of the importance of my job. I began to see that this was the theatre I was playing in and I could be an actor with all the other actors. And with my contribution and my knowledge as an independent – and certainly having that forum in Wodonga, which was a demonstration of the Indi way of working – I had the capacity to really represent my community.

That was a seminal change in my attitude and gave me the confidence that this job could be just as vital as much of the other work I'd done in my life, such as working with women in Papua New Guinea. It was disappointing that in this case it was negative work, stopping things happening rather than making them happen, but I knew that it didn't have to stay that way. In the future, I could be creative, and in the years to come I would be able to make great headway in substantially improving the outlook for tertiary education services in rural and regional Australia.

In my office, we started to talk about the opportunities that this experience opened us up to. As a result, when the next parliament sat, with Malcolm Turnbull as Prime Minister, I was ready with an agenda of things that I wanted to work on for regional Australia. We pulled together a reference group of Indi local governments, the CEOs and mayors, meeting twice a year. They were absolutely hamstrung by the lack of funding. They wanted a policy for regional Australia. It seemed so obvious as a policy goal. I slowly started to realise that the lack of a nationally agreed and implemented regional development policy was not an oversight and that it was part of a strategy – perhaps the National Party didn't want a regional policy, just money it could divvy up and distribute for electoral advantage, something that was played out in the sports-rorts affair in early 2019. Having an overall policy structure would be anathema to that pork-barrelling regime.

But that's getting ahead of things. Suffice to say, I was starting to see a more useful way forward. I could work my position. If I had the community onside, support from the relevant players, and picked the topics I knew about, I could do this job.

Chapter 10

TENDING THE PATCH

While I was learning how to master the fundamentals of being a parliamentarian, I still had tens of thousands of electors to serve. It was a bumpy beginning. In September 2013, having won the election, the next step was moving into the electorate office, which proved to be a complex process. When I arrived, the office at 117 Murphy Street in Wangaratta had no phones, computers or stationery – just some office furniture. And constituents were already knocking at the door. The office had obviously been cleaned out in a hurry. Where to start? Thankfully, some campaign volunteers helped with the transition, setting up constituent files, liaising with Parliamentary Services on protocols, ordering stationery and phones, a thorough clean and decorating the office space with pot plants and a touch of – what else? – orange paint, and a sign at the front. By early October we were open for business. And that Wangaratta office continued to be a busy hub. After six months, I was pleased to also open an office in Wodonga and provide a direct service to the largest population centre in the electorate.

As I saw it, the job of politician had three main parts: representation in parliament, constituent work, and being 'out and about' in the electorate. Of them all, constituent work was a priority; it's where the rubber hits the road in terms of being a representative – of building relationships with the constituents, understanding their issues, solving problems and bringing their voices to parliament. From my perspective, continuing the Indi way of participation and engagement would be predicated on a solid foundation of service to the constituents and encouraging them to take an interest in the work of their MP and what was happening in parliament. Communication and service were paramount, and my staff were my most important resource. They were the ones who daily met with and spoke to constituents, listened to their stories and addressed their issues. I will always be grateful for their dedication, loyalty, professionalism, humanity and willingness to go that extra mile. Thank you, team!

When you're an MP, especially an independent, you rely heavily on the people around you. My staff were my arms, legs and brain. It must be about the team. The working relationships are close. Things go up and down and there can be tensions but also excitement and wonderment. This environment requires a considerable degree of management and one of the people I had to put a lot of work into managing was me. The buck would always stop with me, so I was hypersensitive to anything at all that happened in my office that created an impact outside the office.

At the beginning, there was a fair bit of micromanaging on my part as we got our systems in place and I learnt how to be a boss and how to respond when something went wrong. As a local member, something going wrong can be failing to return a phone call. I would go shopping in Wodonga and be pulled up by a constituent who would tell me how they hadn't got a phone call or they were not happy with something I might or might not have said, and then I'd have to find the right way to follow up.

It took a few trials before we found a system that worked, and I was grateful that there was an increase in the number of staff from the two in the days working with Mr Cameron. I had 12 staff working across three offices, covering the roles of media and communications, diary management and appointments, constituent issues, policy, parliamentary affairs and legislation, community engagement, projects and volunteers, as well as office management, administration, human resources and chief of staff managing a budget close to $300,000. Being an MP was akin to running a small business.

Here's where my business background came to the fore: over time I developed job descriptions for staff, supervision and reporting lines, office policy and procedures, key performance indicators, intra-office communication systems, constituent management protocols, dispute settlement procedures, processes for project planning, implementation, review and continuous improvement, and a yearly strategic plan for the office and electorate. Together with the staff, we developed office administration systems and a policy and procedure manual which I was later able to share with Rebekha Sharkie, Kerryn Phelps and Helen Haines when they were elected, which meant they could hit the ground running without having to manage around the vacuum of an empty office that I had faced.

Making an effective link between the constituent work in the electorate and the representative work in Canberra was also a priority. I attempted to do this in a number of ways: every letter was personally answered, and many were sent on to ministers for formal replies. Staff made appointments with constituents and helped resolve issues, sending me a briefing and, if necessary, details for a phone call. Delegations were arranged to Canberra to meet decision-makers to sort out issues and resolve problems. Where appropriate, and with support from my staff, individuals and groups came to Canberra and did their own advocacy and lobbying. The volunteer program which we called 'back of house' gave an opportunity for any interested constituent to join us in Canberra to experience a parliamentary sitting week.

Every week the Indi Scoop – the office newsletter with a summary of events, speeches, parliamentary news and next week's program – was posted to all media and broadly across the electorate. Quarterly newsletters were sent to every mailbox in the electorate. Across Twitter, Facebook, YouTube and the www.cathymcgowan.com webpage, speeches were posted, discussions facilitated, and opinions generated. And every Friday of a parliamentary sitting week, reporters from the local Indi media – newspapers, radio and TV – would gather in Wodonga for an 'open and frank' media conference. My office was transparent, we were accountable, and we were available.

During the 2013 election campaign, I'd been told by many members of the community that they believed my predecessor in the seat tended not to turn up enough in the electorate and was too focused on the big picture of politics, the larger national issues rather than what was going on in their towns. I resolved to avoid that trap. I would turn up and pay attention to the regional and local detail.

This opened up a host of opportunities for me and my constituents. There were many times when, after hearing from people in Indi about a local issue, I could offer to connect them with a member of the government. The local people for whom I did this were grateful and impressed that not only did I listen but also followed up with action. One example was a community health group that was losing its funding. As well as writing letters, I said, 'Look, why don't you come to Canberra? I'll arrange an appointment and you can talk about your emergency health funding.' My staff arranged passes and took them around Parliament House. They met the relevant advisor, who sorted it out. It had only been a technical hitch, and was able to be resolved on the spot and only by being in Canberra.

There was so much that needed fixing and as a member of parliament I was at long last in a position where I had the opportunity to do something and the capability to open doors. This strategy of facilitating access and opening of doors was driven by necessity to a degree. Because I was not part of the government, I could not be the halfway house for a policy or a program; the government was reluctant to give me money to distribute in my seat but they would give funding to community groups or local government. This added a complication to what I would say to Indi voters. I could rarely say, 'This funding is directly from me'; my job was to explain to the community how funding announcements work: 'If we work together, set up partnerships and build relationships, you will be the beneficiary'. The relevant minister will say 'The Liberal or National party has given you all of this' and that will only be partly true; it will be our partnerships that get results.

Anyone who runs on a platform like mine is automatically inviting intense scrutiny from their electors. Early in the piece, I failed to acknowledge one of my supporters in the supermarket and she wrote a very stern letter admonishing me for not saying 'hello' to her and that clearly I wasn't being my best self and she expected better from me. For her and most of my electorate, being my best self meant turning up, being on time or getting there early, not leaving late, talking to everybody, being my best self in the community context of a representative. It was very rarely about how I behaved in parliament and almost always about how I performed in the community. We had a rule in our office that the turnaround time for a constituent inquiry was 21 days and at one stage we got incredibly busy and missed that

21-day target. I soon started hearing from people when I was out and about that I wasn't being my best self because I had not got back to them. That happened quite a bit, and we had to do a huge amount of work in the office to tighten up our constituent service and response times as it really mattered to each individual.

Occasionally we would get incredibly nasty emails, and it was always challenging to know how best to respond. A phone call often worked, or a carefully crafted reply. Managing disgruntled constituents is an important part of the job, especially if you've won by only 439 votes and you know that the Liberals are going to be coming for you at the next election. I didn't want my staff to have to handle all of that or take the blame for these difficulties, which meant that relationships within the office could become quite complex and needed a lot of attention. While I had a basic understanding of all this from my time as a research assistant and running my consultancy business, it's a different thing when you're always in the public eye.

Fair enough, too. I had used the word 'better' in my campaigning, and I had to deliver. It was difficult work to get the office running efficiently and effectively to meet all the demands. I didn't have time to see every constituent who walked through the door or phoned the office, so we set up strategies for the staff to do the preliminary interview, to sort out the issue and make phone call lists for me. The constituent side of the job is where doing politics differently and better really came into its own. I'd had the experience in Mr Cameron's office and I wanted to be at least as good as him in terms of being able to run an office and deliver for people.

Constituents would come into contact with politics in different ways and many of them were disillusioned, disappointed and distrustful of government. Some wanted action – a visa for a family member or access to social security or help finding accommodation. Others were opinionated about politics and wanted to have a political exchange.

My objective was to make everybody more engaged by giving them an experience of politics that was positive. I wanted to motivate them to become politically interested, if not politically active. For example, a woman came into the office seeking help in getting her employer to pay her superannuation. I wrote a letter to the relevant minister, who wrote back and promised to do something about it. When the woman received a letter from the minister, she was happy. In this type of case, which was far from a one-off in the community, I would also make a speech in parliament, and with permission quote the details outlining the circumstances and call on the government to take more comprehensive action to address the problems. I would send a copy of the speech to the relevant minister and, just as importantly, a copy of the speech with a cover letter to the constituent. Feedback from the constituent in the vast bulk of cases would run along these lines: 'Thank you, Cathy. You might not have solved my problem, but I know you have done your best.'

The most interesting aspect was the expectation that I didn't have to necessarily solve all the problems. I had to hear them and act on them, taking them to the decision-makers. We often got a win. But even when we didn't, constituents were mostly satisfied, knowing that their issue had been taken to Canberra.

One thing that constituents genuinely responded to was seeing themselves and their experiences reflected back to them and acknowledged. In the half-hour before the 2pm start of Question Time, members are permitted to make 90-second speeches. The government and the opposition had a roster for their speeches, and I worked out when I arrived that no-one from the crossbench ever made them. I went to see one of the whips who arrange the speakers' lists and asked how you secured one of those speaking slots, only to be told that it was first come, first served. Eventually, they changed the rules but for my entire first term I would get down to the chamber at 1.15pm; I'd be there first, and I found that over a week I could do four 90-second speeches.

These speeches went straight back to the constituency with a letter from me, and over time I worked out that if I could speak on issues and send the letter back to the Lions Club or schools, I would be talking to larger numbers of constituents with each speech. This worked well: to give voice to so many constituents about an issue they had with government. That was my remit – or part of it, at least.

But one of the most effective steps we took was bringing the people of Indi to experience the inner workings of Canberra politics and parliament through our volunteer program. For most of the people who've never had an experience of government or politics, and especially those who were more cynical about it – and quite a lot were very cynical – this was a way to change their perceptions. Coming to Parliament House or working in the Indi office for a week was open to anybody. The only requirement was to pass the police check. I actively recruited for the program, especially among young people. For those who were dismissive of politics or who had an issue that needed action, I'd encourage them to come up and spend four days during a sitting week – four days is a week in the parliamentary world – and offer to introduce them to the relevant decision-makers or staff. Over time, the program built up a head of steam; during my two terms we had more than 200 volunteers working in the parliamentary office.

Together with the staff, we researched, trialled and developed an induction program with pre-reading that included a map of Parliament House, details about parking and information about parliamentary processes, and at 7.30am on a Monday morning they would arrive at Parliament House and be checked through security. At 8am we would meet for half an hour and I would induct them into how our office worked, discuss values, expectations and behaviours and get to know each other. We went through a 'be your best self' process and emphasised that, while we were in a political environment, big P party politics wasn't our business. They would often want to talk about what the Labor Party or the Liberal Party were doing and I would caution them, 'You can have those opinions, but in this office we leave our Political opinions at the door'. I explained that as an independent I did not do big P Party politics. Of course we would all pay attention, but it wasn't our business. 'What's best for Indi and what's best for the country: that's what we do.' Volunteers would attend the morning staff meeting and staff debrief at the end of the day, so were fully integrated into the office. Often, they were worried about confidentiality and we'd outline the priority of minding our own business and not to mind other people's business. It was liberating and had the effect of de-politicising the office.

It took a while to get the volunteer program to be as good as it could be, and people came to love it. They loved that they had their own voice, that our staff and office were their facilitator to have an active presence in Parliament House. If a volunteer had an issue, one of the staff would work with them to come up with solutions. These were community people – competent and able people who ran organisations, and also many young people who were Year 12 or university students, plus older folks who just wanted to be included and feel they belonged. We would always have projects to do and on a Thursday, which was the last sitting day of the week, I would usually make a 90-second speech about their work. Some of the local councils in Indi used the volunteer program as a professional development activity for a director or manager. This was valuable for both parties, and the spin-off was that the staff would take what they'd learnt back to their councils, and when councillors subsequently came to Canberra to do their lobbying they were well briefed on procedures.

I was careful not to make too much of a fuss about the volunteers coming up each week. I did my 90-second speeches, of course, but I tried to keep the program under the rug as much as I could, as I suspected that if the government could shut it down, they would. Eventually, there was some minor curtailment on the allocation of passes. But my staff had a good relationship with the Pass Office and with the Speaker's office and we were able to manage around the changes. Everywhere they went, the volunteers created goodwill with the staff in Parliament House.

The volunteer program was one part of the job that kept me sane and happy. Talking about and showing interested members of my community how democracy worked was often the highlight of my week. I would be asked 'How can you put up with all these people around all the time?' and I'd tell them, 'Really, it's the part of the job that I love, having good community people in parliament; they are learning about how the system works, giving me their feedback, actively lessening their cynicism, and they return home more engaged, and usually keen to take on a leadership role'. Maybe also it's the teacher in me coming to the fore. And it encouraged me to be my best self, and a daily reminder of who I was working for. When we started the week with the volunteer induction, it kept me and my staff mindful of the values of our office – of not being Political and not judging people on their Politics, truly to be of an open and independent persuasion.

There were many issues that came through the doors of the electorate office and during listening posts as part of the valley visits, which had local as well as national impacts; and the Indi reference groups – sometimes morphing into action groups – became our way of building partnerships, enabling engagement and action. In later chapters I refer to the work of Totally Renewable Indi which was our reference group on climate action and to the Indi Telecommunication Action Group which achieved great results on the mobile phone towers, and here briefly I would like to acknowledge the work of the Border Rail Action Group (BRAG).

The Border Rail Action Group, based around Albury and Wodonga, came together out of frustration with the slow progress on repairing the north east train line. They were diligent in their research and advocacy and extremely knowledgeable about how the Australian Rail Track Corporation (ARTC) and the Victorian, New South Wales and Commonwealth governments all operated their train lines. They were persistent and dedicated. From the first they made full use of all the opportunities to come to Canberra. Initially as volunteers in my office, they arranged deputations and drafted questions for senators seeking details on the operations of the ARTC and its spending, planning and consultation.

With their encouragement I presented private members bills, moved motions and asked questions seeking more information about the holdups and plans for improvement. Their confidence and resilience grew with each visit to Canberra, and when the first $100 million was announced in the 2017 budget no group was more deserving of acknowledgment than BRAG. When an additional $135 million was invested the following year as part of the Sydney–Melbourne inland freight system, they went to work with the engineers on design, planning and consultation processes and, happily for the community of Indi, the BRAG team continue to maintain their watchful eye on the ARTC and its spending.

Of all the issues, our poor relationship with Australia's First Nations people continues to puzzle me. While we did make some progress in Indi, I was continually frustrated by the slow pace and the lack of resources available for action.

Having made an apology speech to Aboriginal and Torres Strait Islander people on behalf of the community of Indi early in my parliamentary term, I also made speeches on relevant occasions and met with individuals and groups representing them. I was particularly grateful to minister Ken Wyatt for the two visits he made to the electorate where he met with Elders and representatives of Aboriginal organisations and allied services. However it wasn't until Malcolm Turnbull appointed me to the Joint Select Committee on Constitutional Recognition of Aboriginal and Torres Strait Islander Peoples that I truly came to understand the extent of the task in front of us as a community and a nation, to create a meaningful voice, and a just treaty backed by rigorous truth telling. As I write this in 2020, I am pleased that Helen Haines has committed to continue this work.

Chapter 11

MAKE SOME NOISE

I was elected because the people of Indi wanted to be respected and connected. The three things they were looking for were having a responsive local member who would show up and focus on their concerns, a reliable mobile phone network service that wasn't full of black spots and equal to what people in the city took for granted, and an improved train service that did not leave them feeling left out and isolated. From day one, in 2013 after being declared the MP for Indi, along with my staff and the Voices for Indi group, I set about trying to give the community the heightened level of respect that it desired – and deserved. But I also had to get something happening on telecommunications. I struggled to find a way to do this.

In the country, Telstra is mainly responsible for mobile phone infrastructure, with Optus looking after some as well. These are private companies. The government's role was always a bit opaque, although I could see that it was crucial. The minister for communications was Malcolm Turnbull and his department influenced and often determined outcomes on the mobile network through its spending programs. Turnbull was busy at the time, working away on remaking the National Broadband Network that the previous government had established. I needed to get him to commit to improving our mobile phone tower network in Indi. Most of the communities in Indi are a long way from each other, up to 70 per cent of the electorate is either state or national parks, the area is bushfire prone and much is alpine country. For the people in Indi, it was a matter of equity, safety, business and tourism. How could I get these phone towers?

My own community and one of the staff in Turnbull's office showed me the way. In Mansfield, a beautiful town that is the entry point to the southern snowfields, the mobile coverage was appalling. It's very hilly territory, a holiday destination with large numbers of tourists coming through, and the situation was intolerable, so a group of citizens, helped by the local council, set up a telecommunications action group. The chair of the group was an ex-telco executive and was overseeing an impressive operation. I had a briefing with the group and its action plan was exactly what I needed. It outlined how the system worked and how to get the Telcos to pay attention. Mansfield needed a plan, which meant bringing in partners, including the emergency service providers who are so important in country locations. It also explained the technical aspects including the difference a properly placed tower on a hill could make.

This was the information that I needed and I began to put together, with support from the Mansfield team, a similar organisation for the entire electorate, the Indi Telecommunications Action Group. Each of the councils in Indi sent a representative, and over time, using the Mansfield model, they all agreed to tip in some money – my office put in $2,000 – so that we could employ a consultant to work with each of the local councils on determining the priority locations for new towers.

The Department of Communications had made $100 million available for mobile towers, and when that grant round opened, Indi was organised. We had done the work and the nine local councils weren't squabbling. They had each sent me a list of their top three locations.

They knew what to do because the Indi Telecommunications Action Group had organised a forum with the local telco providers and department people who travelled to Indi from Canberra to explain the funding program and outline the guidelines and criteria.

One of the lessons for me was that even if, in Indi, we might not have had a lot of skilled individuals with expert knowledge on specific issues like this, we did have a few. If you could find them and offer a personal invitation to work on bodies like the action group, they would usually agree to come on board.

Consequently, we set up a range of community-based Indi reference groups, often local government-connected, made up of people with special expertise. As a rule, they would meet at my office three or four times a year. To my knowledge, that had not happened before, largely because of the geography. Thanks to the valleys that were so much a feature of our area, the degree of isolation was marked and this in turn had encouraged parochialism within many of the local councils.

What we were doing, quite consciously, was trying to establish an Indi brand – again something new – that gave us a stronger, more cohesive face to the rest of the world but also made those of us who lived and worked in the electorate feel like we were part of something bigger and more effective. This way of working added to what we were beginning to describe as 'the Indi way': community engagement, linking up to one level of government and down to another level of government, informed and driven by participation, networking and action.

On the mobile phone towers, I had the local part sorted out but what about the rest? The way I saw it, the $100 million the government was offering was not actually a political grant program; it went through the department, but how did the department set up its checklist? I sought advice around my contacts in Parliament House. The feedback was that I was being naïve in thinking this was all about the department and that 'of course the minister's office would be involved'. I was advised to get in touch with Malcolm Turnbull's office and get to know his staff and make sure that he, as the minister, understood what I was trying to do. I took a couple of my staff to a meeting and he allocated one of his staff to be our main point of contact. I also requested a departmental briefing to make sure we were fully across all the details and established relationships with the decision-makers.

Over the next couple of years, our staff had regular contact. In that first meeting in Malcolm Turnbull's office I asked the staffer for guidance on how the decision about funding was made. He looked at me and pointed at a pile of printouts on his desk. 'Cathy, see in front of me? That's today's media monitor list. If you really want to make an impact you've got to get into that.' I could hear the practicality of it but I thought, 'How do I, an independent backbencher from country Victoria, get into media monitors when it's largely population-based – predominantly big city talkback and their media?' Obviously, I was giving him a quizzical look. He said, 'Basically you've got to make a noise'. I thought making a noise was speaking in parliament and writing letters to the minister. He said, 'No, you've got to get into this pile. You've got to make a noise.' I came out of that meeting informed and transformed.

This inspired a real change in my way of working with my communities and particularly the reference groups. I checked out what media got into the minister's media monitoring file, which for our purposes was material from *The Border Mail* and the regional ABC. When I got back home, I talked with my staff and with the local government people about how we would go about making noise. If we wanted to score big on mobile phone towers, we had to demonstrate community engagement and community involvement. That translated to money: the community had to put in something like $10,000 per tower and the local councils weren't overjoyed about that but they did it. And then I experimented in making noise.

The remote village of Dartmouth, established in the 1970s as a settlement for workers constructing the Dartmouth Dam, was home to about 45 people with an old copper telephone line that regularly broke down and their phone service was very poor. I'd written letters to Telstra about it before without result, the explanation being that the NBN was coming, so there was no point in repairing the line. I wasn't sure the NBN would ever make it to Dartmouth, but I couldn't afford to wait around to find out. I contacted the local TV news and the local paper *The Border Mail*, and asked Malcolm Turnbull a question about Dartmouth's poor telecommunications service in the House. On the same day, the Dartmouth people had a community meeting in the pub, which was covered by *The Border Mail*. We had also arranged talkback radio coverage in Albury–Wodonga. A week later, I went back to the regional manager of Telstra and he reported that he'd had a call from headquarters with instructions to fix Dartmouth. I realised that was what noise looked like. Our strategy had worked.

From then on, the people from the Indi Telecommunications Action Group inundated the local papers with letters and stories about how poor their mobile coverage was. My staff bundled up all the newspaper articles and I sent them with a letter along the lines of 'Dear Malcolm, we've got problems with Cudgewa, there's been a road accident, there was no mobile phone coverage, someone almost died. Here are the stories from the newspaper. Could your department please investigate what happened about this?' I was amplifying the noise.

This was such a lightbulb moment, when I understood that it wasn't enough to be an independent, and to have made the seat marginal and competitive. Now I needed to use my voice and the community's voice. After that realisation I set about finding every possible way of making noise in the system. I'd encouraged our office volunteers to make noise about their issues when they returned home and encourage others in their community to make noise too. If that staffer hadn't told me about noise, I would never have understood it.

The noise and the community work produced great results. I managed to be there in a parliamentary committee room when Malcolm Turnbull announced who had got the grants for the towers. I hadn't been invited but I found out through our parliament network not long before it started. The department had put up big maps, with the parts of Australia that were getting the towers coloured in pink. As I walked in, I bumped into Rob Harris, who had been a reporter in our district, and was now in the press gallery. He said, 'Wow, Indi did well out of this', and I thought he was being sarcastic. I thought, 'Oh, that's terrible; well, maybe if I get one tower, that would be okay'. Then someone handed me a map and I saw that a large section of Indi's valleys were covered in pink. Later, I discovered that we had done extraordinarily well. After parts of Western Australia, our electorate had won the most towers in the country.

This happened while Tony Abbott was prime minister, before September 2015, when Malcolm Turnbull replaced him, and I'll briefly reflect on these two men. (In my two terms, there was a third prime minister, Scott Morrison – a remarkable rate of turnover.) On paper, it might have been assumed that I would be well disposed to Tony Abbott. We were both raised as observant and dedicated Catholics, not just in our families but within the very disciplined and often demanding Catholic education system. But by the time the 2013 election came around, one that Abbott was set to win well before election day, I was no fan of him as a politician. I didn't like his attitude to politics, which I found personally aggressive, and I did not like his lack of respect for Julia Gillard. He seemed to have a problem with promoting women to his front bench.

I did not personally dislike Tony Abbott either before or after I entered parliament – there was no room for that in my way of approaching politics – but I can't say that I liked him either. It was just that he went about being the Liberal Party's leader, both in opposition and as prime minister, the wrong way, as far as I could see. Too little humanity, too little humility and far too much Politics. Above all, it was his position on climate change that appalled me.

I developed a more favourable opinion of Malcolm Turnbull. He was not prime minister when we got our phone towers. But from the outset, whenever I had dealings with him, I found him to be honourable, respectful and interested in me and Indi. He did not seem to view me through a political prism. I had been wanting to get my photo taken with Tony Abbott since I had arrived in parliament, to signal to my electorate that here I was, their member in the place where the prime minister is. Abbott initially agreed to a photo but continually fobbed me off and it wasn't happening. Other ministers had given me the same treatment. Contrast that with Malcolm Turnbull: after the mobile tower announcement I asked him if we could get a photo together and he did not hesitate to say 'yes'. We stood together for the photographer and he said, 'Congratulations, Indi has done really well here, and you did no deals'. A big difference. When he became prime minister, I was relieved, and we went on to forge a positive working relationship.

Winning funding for those new phone towers represented a big achievement for Indi. We had delivered. But politics of a pretty nasty type was something that I also had to come to terms with during my first term. The very worst experience I had during my time as the member for Indi was the pursuit of the young people, the Indi expats who had been instrumental in the beginnings of Voices for Indi and our whole political adventure.

A year after the election, I was contacted by Hedley Thomas, a journalist with *The Australian*, who wanted to talk about what he said was fraudulent activity around my volunteers. The issue was the authenticity of their electoral enrolments and whether they were legally entitled to vote in Indi. There had been a formal complaint. I was stunned. Seriously, this warranted investigation by a national newspaper? Obviously they thought it did, because stories started to appear, suggesting that people such as my nephew Ben, who had moved to Darwin for work, had been engaged in voter fraud. Thus began the saga of the 'Indi 27' and what I still regard as a dreadful pursuit of citizens, who were merely exercising their civic right to bring about political change, by the Liberal Party, one part of the media and the Australian Federal Police.

The '27' comes from the number of young activists who, according to ultimately unfounded allegations by their accusers, were supposedly helping me get elected and casting a vote for me when they did not live in Indi and thus should not have been able to influence the outcome in 2013. It was the dirtiest of grubby politics and a major case of sour grapes. I knew I had won fair and square, and these young people had done nothing wrong. In fact, they had followed all the rules. What had happened was that someone – maybe a team, we still don't know – attached to the Liberal Party had trawled through social media posts to identify supporters who had advocated for me and then apparently cross-checked their electoral address against their residential address. This was not real-world stuff. Country kids keep their permanent residential address as 'home', even though they might be living temporarily in Melbourne or attending university. When the 2013 election got underway, many of my supporters who had been living in Melbourne had finished their studies and had moved off to Darwin or Sydney or somewhere else, but they still kept their residential address at home. The Australian Electoral Commission website allowed for such a thing. It said: 'Students living away from home can be enrolled at their permanent address'.

The AFP began an investigation of the 27 young people. It took a terrible emotional toll on all of them. Eventually two young women were charged with giving false or misleading information to the Australian Electoral Commission, an offence that carried a maximum jail term of one year. The AFP wasted thousands of hours, not to mention dollars, poking around in the private lives of my supporters, interviewing their landlords, parents, employers and friends. And it was all for nothing. In April 2016, just three months out from the federal election, the charges against the two young women were dropped after prosecutors determined they had acted within the law by voting in Indi.

My reflection on this low point of my time as an MP? I'd long suspected that the Liberal Party was going to come after me when I won the seat. They had the reputation as poor losers. This investigation began when Tony Abbott was prime minister and it seemed in keeping with the way he did politics. Sophie Mirabella was determined to win Indi back and she was preselected to run again in June 2015, a few months before Malcolm Turnbull took over. Our campaign people knew that some elements of the government were not being benevolent and we knew that they could be vindictive. We were conscious of that in our first campaign and it was a risk we often spoke about, that we would get pushback for trying to wrest the seat away from the Liberals. People feared they would lose contracts, be blacklisted if they showed support for an independent and were scared of the retribution they would experience from showing public support. We weren't naïve about the downside that might follow our community organising but the extent of it was disappointing to say the least.

But I also knew that their approach had the potential to create problems for the Liberal Party. I had a clear track record for my honesty. I had been rigorous in running my business properly and with good governance. I had served on a range of boards of local church, farming and banking organisations and had a reputation not only for following the letter of the law but also paying attention to detail. I hoped that it would be hard to bring a case against me. I suppose the Liberals thought that trying to crush the reputations of my young supporters, who had fewer resources with which to defend themselves, would be an effective way of putting a shot across the bows of anybody else who wanted to do what we had done.

The episode ultimately hurt the Liberal Party in Indi. Many people in the community were shocked at seeing the names of the young people being used in this way in the papers. They all had families, networks and friends who worked away from home and this issue impacted on a much larger group than me or my extended family. By examining the multiplier effect, a large number of individuals and families across northeast Victoria could possibly be also affected. These people were offended. They could see that this was not fair, and they could work out that it had not come out of the blue.

As the Indi 27 affair was coming to an end in 2016, I found myself involved in – well, not really involved in, but a witness to – an unfortunate episode that did lead to a highly publicised court action involving my political competitor Sophie Mirabella. After I had made my first speech in the House, the Liberal backbencher Ken Wyatt, a proud Aboriginal man, came over to congratulate me. He admired my handmade brooch, given to me for the occasion by Aboriginal people from my electorate, and offered to work with me. We got to know each over the next two years, and by early 2016 he was assistant minister for aged care and Aboriginal health and had met with people from our local Aboriginal health service. This led to him agreeing to open Cooinda, an aged-care home in Benalla in April, three months out from the next election. As the local member, I was invited, and Sophie, as the Liberal Party candidate, also found her way there.

As the former member, Sophie worked the room as she knew a lot of the people. Minister Wyatt was there in an official capacity and so was I as the local MP. We had a good relationship, and I wanted a photo with him, just as I'd had my picture taken with Malcolm Turnbull when he announced the mobile phone towers. I asked his staff if we could get one and they agreed that we could have it taken next to the plaque marking the official opening. Sophie intervened, confronting Ken and advising him that it was not politically wise to go ahead with the photo, given that he was a Liberal and I was an independent, and he moved away. It was all a bit difficult. On my way home that night, a journalist from the *Benalla Ensign*, Libby Price, called. She had not been at the function. She asked, 'Did Sophie Mirabella push you?' I didn't want to get involved. I said, 'Look, I can't talk to you about it. An incident happened. I can't talk about it.'

The paper then published a story that said Sophie had pushed me away from Ken Wyatt. This report was picked up by other papers and news services and caused a stir far beyond the boundaries of Indi. As it started to rage through the media, I rang Ken, who was on his way to New York, and he just wanted it to go away. He told me he would rather I didn't talk about it because if I did it would blow up further. So, at his request, I refused to answer questions about it. The paper published a correction six months after the original article that acknowledged that I had not been pushed. But that was not the end of it. Sophie sued the owners of the *Benalla Ensign* and its editor and, when the case was heard in the County Court in 2018, I was called as a witness. Minister Wyatt was too, and he told the court that Sophie had placed her hands on his chest as she urged him not to get a photo taken with me. Technically not a push. A six-member jury found for Sophie and she was awarded $175,000 in damages.

As the 2016 campaign started to move into gear, Voices for Indi was in good shape. We had more volunteers, more money, a better operation, the hubs were restarted, and we had much more visibility and recognition. Orange was no longer a novelty: it was the political look of Indi. We had runs on the board. The mobile phone towers had been secured and our responsiveness to constituents was widely recognised. But the Liberal Party were determined to make me a flash in the pan, an aberration, and they were throwing big resources into their campaign.

My public presentation was still a bit 'unpolished', no more so than at an event at Wangaratta's Pinsent Hotel. Sky News host Paul Murray was doing a series of live broadcasts in marginal seats, where the candidates would debate and take questions from the audience. I had never done a live broadcast before and I was not looking forward to it, but I had to be there. For all our improved campaigning skills, we didn't know how to prepare for such an event. Although four or five of the other candidates were there, this was billed as a Cathy versus Sophie showdown. This might have suited Sophie but it wasn't my natural environment.

We'd put the word out to supporters about the broadcast, but we hadn't activated a large crowd. When I walked into the Pinsent Hotel with five of my staff and half a dozen volunteers, the place was full of Sophie supporters. There were about 100 people there. They were angry with me about the Wyatt incident and there was some jostling and a lot of bad feeling.

Prior to going, I'd been at a community meeting at the Wangaratta hospital, where annual awards were being given to staff. I was sitting next to the chairman of Northeast Health Wangaratta, Brendan Schutt, who told me he would be joining the debate audience and he planned to ask a question. During the broadcast, Sophie went in hard with an argument that whatever spending I had secured for Indi was not down to me, it was due to the government – that is, her fellow Liberals. The audience cheered her every syllable and grumbled and hissed when I made my points. I was getting pretty distressed. Then Brendan asked his question, which related to the Wangaratta hospital's redevelopment plans. We both supported the redevelopment but Sophie added this reflection on the 2013 outcome: 'I had a commitment for a $10 million allocation to the Wangaratta hospital that, if elected, I was going to announce the week after the election. That is $10 million that Wangaratta hasn't had because Cathy got elected. So the question is: who can best deliver that funding in a Turnbull Coalition government? It's about who has the ability and the knowledge and the contacts in government to go to the top of the list. Cathy wasn't able to do it: I will be.'

Her answer did not cause a stir when she gave it. I scuttled away as quickly as I could, as I felt my performance had been poor. Our team hadn't understood what we were up against and I assumed we had lost the debate. In fact, I felt I'd been thrashed. I drove towards home, despondent. It was late at night. Then my phone started buzzing with notifications. I pulled over to take a look and Sophie's answer about the $10 million that Indi didn't get had taken off on Twitter. Barrie Cassidy, with his 168,000 followers, who came from Chiltern, not far from Indigo Valley, had been watching and had highlighted her response.

By the time I got to work the next day, her statement was a big deal: the electorate missing out on $10 million because people had voted the wrong way was a national story and it wasn't hurting me, it was hurting the Liberal campaign. But still I knew that I should have been better prepared and could never jeopardise the hard work of Voices for Indi like that again. I asked Judy Brewer for advice and she put me in touch with a professional media coach who gave me some very tough, and incredibly valuable, media training. And I realised that if we were going to win this election, it really was about Sophie and me. While that tussle had been going on during the 2013 election it had always been subtle, it was not front and centre. This time it was a clear choice. The old way or the new: Sophie and the Liberal party and their way of doing things, or Cathy and the community. We were campaigning about the here and now and the Liberals were still fighting the previous election. That defined the contest.

Not only did the campaign focus on the two personalities, my parliamentary voting record was used as a weapon of attack. Because I believe that man-made climate change is real and I sat on the crossbench, the Liberals tried to portray me as a newer version of Tony

Windsor and Rob Oakeshott, who had given Labor a majority in the previous parliament. The Liberal campaign made up posters to that effect, featuring a very ugly black and white photo of me and Bill Shorten, declaring that I voted with the Greens and Labor in the parliament. Rationally, this was ridiculous, but I believe it had a notable negative effect on my vote. A lot of rural people have a deep dislike for 'greenies', which I've never understood because 90 per cent of the farmers I know are fully engaged with protecting the environment. I met an older farming woman in Wodonga one day and she said, 'Oh Cathy, I can't vote for you'. I asked why and she told me, 'I just can't, you know. You're really nice and I knew your mum and your dad but you're just too Green.' Just making the accusation was enough to shift the perceptions of some people.

On election night, 2 July 2016, Voices for Indi set up in the Wangaratta Town Hall. The tally board was operating and one of the Indi expats, Cam Klose, picked it early in the night. He came over to me, excited, and said, 'You're gonna win this, we're gonna win this'. And we did. It was not like 2013: there was no agonising wait for the next week or more, no scrambling for scrutineers. We knew we had won on the night. My primary vote climbed 3.5 per cent to 34.7. The National Party ran a candidate this time, who picked up 17.2 per cent of the vote. Sophie's primary vote fell correspondingly by almost the same amount – 17 per cent. Enough of those quiet National Party voters who had backed me in 2013 had stayed with me to help get me over the line again. After preferences, we had built on our margin, taking 54.8 of the preferred voted. We were entrenching Indi as a marginal, highly contested seat, which was what we had set out to do. Even so, I believe – and our campaign people who are more numerate than me share this view – that the 'Cathy is a greenie' attacks probably shaved about two points off my vote; the negative feedback we were getting in the last couple of weeks, driven by the Liberal attack ads, certainly suggested this.

It was a good night for us, but a bittersweet night for Malcolm Turnbull. There was a swing to Labor and his parliamentary majority was in danger. An angry Turnbull said he expected to be able to continue to govern but there would need to be more counting. The crossbench was about to come into its own.

Malcolm rang me on the Sunday morning. He said the numbers on the floor of the House were not yet crystal clear, but he still wanted to talk to me in the following week. It was exciting because I was in a much stronger place than in 2013. Having won so well in Indi, I was confident that I had my community backing me. We had been upfront about how we were going to do business and I knew I had a really clear way forward. All that preparation and workshopping we'd done with the staff and volunteers about how we were going to be in the community and how we were going to answer questions about a balance of power situation meant that I could say to the Prime Minister on that 11am phone call, 'Malcolm, I'm not going to do any deals with you. I'll treat every piece of legislation on its merits.'

Chapter 12

IS THIS THE BEST OUR POLITICS CAN BE?

The official national count of the 2016 results dragged on for more than a week amid some mild uncertainty about the outcome as the count in several seats was sorted. In truth, it was pretty clear on election night that Malcolm Turnbull was right to predict that his government would remain in power, with a slim majority being a more likely outcome than a minority situation. Nine days after the election, Bill Shorten conceded that Labor could not win and ultimately the Coalition commanded a one-seat majority in the House of Representatives.

But the 45th parliament was, by modern standards, one of the most fractious and unstable Australia has seen. The result in the 150-seat lower house was the government had 76 seats, Labor had 69, with a crossbench of five, which included two independents: Andrew Wilkie from Tasmania and me. In the Senate, the result was even more varied and uncertain, with a crossbench of 20, meaning that the government had to get nine extra votes to pass legislation. And that was the way it was at the outset.

Deeper into the term, questions over the eligibility of a range of MPs to sit in both houses because of their citizenship status created a chaotic parliament, leading to six lower house by-elections. And then in late 2018, after Malcolm Turnbull resigned from parliament upon losing the leadership, Kerryn Phelps won his seat and another independent joined the crossbench ranks, meaning that Scott Morrison found himself leading a minority government.

In the days after the election, that was all ahead of us, of course, but it's useful to bear in mind because it gives a sense of how the instability and uncertainty that marked politics right from the start accelerated the longer the term went on – and how much my role as an independent changed. In my first term, as far as the government was concerned, I was largely incidental because its big majority meant that I could not affect outcomes on the floor of the House, where governments are made and can be unmade. In the second term, that looked unlikely to be the case, hence the prime minister's Sunday morning phone call.

I had been preparing for this possibility. The 2016 election was long and gruelling for all concerned. The initial burst of enthusiasm that had been evident in the polls after Abbott was replaced by Turnbull had faded and Labor was increasingly competitive. It was looking to be a tight election contest and that inevitably led to me being asked many times as the election approached what I would do in the event of a hung parliament. This had been asked of me before the 2013 election too, but it was largely academic because everyone knew that the Coalition would not have to worry about its numbers in the lower house. This time, though, there was good reason for people to want to know. To sharpen my thinking on this, I talked to Andrew Wilkie.

Andrew was my fellow independent in the House. He was one of the most skilled political and parliamentary operators around the place and we spoke regularly. Andrew had won his seat in Tasmania from the Labor Party in 2010, and he was wise about how the party machines work and how they run campaigns, so I was keen to learn from him and his team. He gave us good advice, which we followed.

His insight was that an independent needed to have a small nimble team, because the big parties were run out of the city and they were cumbersome – overburdened by rules and their larger size. Being nimble meant you could act on things quickly and change direction when desirable.

Andrew said that whenever he was asked what he would do if there was a hung parliament, with neither side holding a majority and thus needing crossbench support in order to convince the governor-general it had the confidence of the House, he ruled out any deals altogether as an ironclad position. He would look at every piece of legislation on its merits and he was not going to prejudge who he would support in parliament. I would push him, 'But how can that work? What about a guarantee of confidence? Who will you give confidence to?' His response was, 'I'm certainly not going to make that decision now. I'll wait and see what confidence means, and what the numbers look like and the quality of the person and the team, and I'll make that decision at the time. But my vote will not be bought.' This seemed exactly the right position to take. We knew how much damage had been done to Rob Oakeshott and Tony Windsor over what was seen as their deal with Julia Gillard. I picked up Andrew's position.

Our team had done a wonderful job during the 2016 campaign. The Liberal and Coalition candidates had really given us a tough time, but we hadn't just won, we'd won well. And now we had moved up the pecking order a little bit and could hopefully use that prominence to secure some more wins for Indi. Personally, although I was happy and thankful for the renewed endorsement by a majority of my constituents – even overwhelmed by it – in my head I knew I had fought my last election and that this would be my last term; six years would be enough and I wanted to return to my old life. That decision was liberating. I would work hard, using what I had learnt, and I would not be daunted in the way that I had been when I first entered the parliament three years earlier. And dealing one-on-one with the prime minister, discussing the future of his government, was my first assignment.

We met at the Commonwealth Government offices at Melbourne's Treasury Place on the Friday after the election, three days before Bill Shorten conceded. Although the progressive vote count favoured the government, this meeting was a little bit of insurance for the prime minister. It was an exciting time, for me at least. We were not strangers; our offices had worked together on the mobile phone towers when he was the minister, and I'd always been impressed by his staff and their open attitude. I thought he oversaw a good, professional operation and he was always willing to have a conversation and a cup of tea.

I had prepared a statement and told him I would be making no deals, that I would continue to work with the government of the day to achieve what's needed for my electorate and the nation, and I would consider each piece of legislation on its merits and vote according to my conscience. He thought that was fine and we agreed that on confidence motions I would listen to the arguments. I confirmed to him that I would continue my practice of supporting the government on supply. We talked some more about general political issues and agreed that we would have an open and frank relationship.

Although all of my dealings with Bill Shorten had been good – in fact, he made it his business to offer me comfort and support when the Indi 27 nonsense blew up – and he and his Party had fought a fair and respectful campaign in Indi, I was not unhappy that Malcolm Turnbull had squeaked back in. I was very relieved it was not Tony Abbott with whom I was having that discussion. I had always been concerned that if the balance of power came my way I'd have to work with Abbott and in all conscience, with his values and behaviours, I'm not sure I could have done it. In contrast, Malcolm Turnbull always struck me as a man of his word.

After Turnbull finished his meeting with me, he was heading off to the electorate of Chisholm in Melbourne's southeast to go on a street walk with its new Liberal member, Julia Banks. Chisholm was the only seat the Liberals took from Labor at the election, which made all the difference for the government, giving it the crucial vote it needed to maintain a parliamentary majority. I didn't know Julia then, but got to know her towards the end of 2018 after she left the Liberal Party and joined the crossbench. I recall watching a happy Turnbull walking off to his rendezvous in Chisholm with Julia and thinking 'He is comfortable with strong women and what a decent prime minister he is', and I looked forward to working with him.

But his happiness would not last for long. He was, and is, an incredibly self-assured man but he was up against strong forces in the two years that followed before he resigned after a failed challenge by Peter Dutton destroyed his leadership, paving the way for Scott Morrison to swoop in, seemingly from nowhere. He was regularly white-anted by Abbott and the large number of intractable climate-change deniers in the Coalition party room. And the citizenship problem caused by the wording of section 44 of the Constitution played merry hell throughout the parliament, forcing by-elections involving members from four parties – the Liberals, the Nationals, the ALP and the Nick Xenophon Team (later the Centre Alliance). Some will argue that he could have more skilfully handled his climate-change problems but few, if any, seem to be able to explain exactly how he could have done that. The wafer-thin nature of the government's majority made it hard for him to stand up to anyone inside the Coalition. And the section 44 problem could hardly be laid at his feet.

We met every few months after the election and every two weeks when parliament was sitting. I did not have to go chasing after him. He would send me a text: 'Cathy, is it time for us to have a cup of tea?' He would tell me after his first phone call to Donald Trump how relieved he was that his deal with Barack Obama to resettle some of our refugees in America had survived the presidential transition, although, famously, it was touch and go for a few minutes during the call. The frequency of our meetings, and the interaction between his office and mine, increased throughout 2017 as the government's political position started to get shaky. The government was not travelling well in the polls and when the Nationals leader Barnaby Joyce was forced to a by-election over his eligibility to sit in the parliament, followed soon by the Liberal member for Bennelong, John Alexander, Turnbull made a different sort of approach to me.

One big policy initiative I did want to get the government to act on was an all-embracing national policy for regional Australia. I had talked with Turnbull about this. He supported it but the policy formulation process needed to start somewhere. Andrew Robb as a minister until 2016 had succeeded with a policy for northern Australia, so I followed his model; begin with an inquiry, then a green paper, then a white paper, then a fully developed policy that would take in all of regional Australia. I was a member of the select committee established as the first step in the process and we were travelling around the country hearing submissions.

In November 2017, when I arrived in Darwin, where the committee was set to hold hearings, there were half a dozen missed calls from the prime minister on my phone. When I returned his call, he had a big question: 'Would I consider replacing Tony Smith as the Speaker?' There had been some media speculation that this might happen, but I'd dismissed it and didn't expect it to lead to an offer. His reasoning was simple: the government was in trouble with its numbers and Smith is a Liberal, so he would return to the government benches and add an extra certain vote while moving me into that more impartial role.

I noted the conversation but put it in the back of my mind because I was fully committed to the regional development inquiry and we had hearings and investigations to conduct. A few days later, Turnbull called again. This time we talked for half an hour and he laid out his plans for the next sitting where we could get up a federal anti-corruption commission and the national regional and rural policy. He knew which policy buttons to press to try to win me over, and he flattered me, telling me I would be a good Speaker and here was my opportunity to maintain good governance in the House. I thanked him and said I would think about it. And then I went into a panic.

I owed it to him, as prime minister, to consider this question seriously. He'd dealt with me decently and he had never asked me for anything else, and the Speaker's position was a big deal. I could see how I could solve his problem with numbers and keep the government steady but at what price to me and Voices for Indi? I spoke with my senior staff and trusted advisors, seeking their advice. They reminded me that I was the one who wasn't going to do any deals. When I rang to decline his offer, he was overseas. I told him the truth: I didn't do deals and I would like our current relationship to continue. I explained that part of my decision-making was that I couldn't imagine going back to Indi and telling the people who'd voted for me as an independent that I'd sold out, that I had given up my voice in parliament and with it my ability to represent them. I'd campaigned as an independent, an honest voice speaking up for Indi. As Speaker, I'd no longer be able to vote and would lose that voice. How could I represent my community without having a voice in parliament?

This was about much more than just my reputation. I had already booked my ticket for my trip back to civilian life come the end of this second term and one of my most important responsibilities was to ensure that our movement was in the best possible working order ahead of the 2019 election. Taking the high-paying, high-profile job of Speaker would almost certainly have blown up the Voices for Indi enterprise; you could imagine the argument against the candidate running as my successor – that Voices for Indi was just as much a part of the degraded self-interest that often characterised the behaviour of the big parties.

Delivering on what we had promised at the outset in 2013 always had to remain my core mission. Getting the mobile towers in the first term was a good start and seemed to be enough to win favour in 2016 but in the second term it was imperative that something substantial happened on that other big connectivity-related need in Indi: a long-overdue improvement in our train service. Fortunately, in the first post-election budget there was some movement, with a $100 million allocation for the Northeast train line in the 2017 budget. After that, together with BRAG I worked hard to establish partnerships with the federal and Victorian governments and the Australian Rail Track Corporation to find more funding to fix up the train line. And it worked: another $135 million. The process of winning funding for the train line was a good example of how being an independent works and the effectiveness of building strategic partnerships, badgering decision-makers and making noise.

IS THIS THE BEST OUR POLITICS CAN BE?

In October 2019, I visited Canberra to receive an integrity award from the Accountability Round Table, named in honour of the late Victorian Liberal senator Alan Missen, chiefly for my advocacy for a national integrity commission. I used the opportunity to speak to different members of parliament to revive a campaign to get the remaining refugees removed from Manus Island, which had long been a goal of mine as an MP. I met some of the staffers who had been involved, and in passing I mentioned how wonderful it had been to get that $100 million for the train line. One of them laughed and said, 'Do you know how that happened?' I didn't and she explained, 'There was X million dollars in the transport budget sitting there, and we gave you $100 million, we gave another member $100 million and somebody else got $100 million'. I said, 'Really, it was an arbitrary allocation of money?' and she said, 'Well, you'd absolutely been on our back all the time. We needed to get you off our back.' Lesson being: if you want money for the trains in your electorate, get on their back, be a bloody nuisance and they'll find $100 million for you ... but first make sure your seat is marginal and, even better, elect an independent MP.

The money for the train line and the mobile phone towers were such clear deliverables, especially in Indi's rural and farming communities, which was where I really needed to build my credibility, given that I had solid backing in Indi's bigger towns. The point here was that it wasn't just me jumping up and down trying to get the money. The people of Indi got organised, became strategic and put up plans. Everything we argued for was properly thought-out and based on a genuine need. There was no political taint.

During my time in parliament there were several issues affecting the electorate where the national response was, in my opinion, simply not adequate and I found this deeply frustrating. Climate change was a national problem, and the crossbench raised it consistently in parliament, but, apart from the Abbott government's early work in undoing the carbon tax legislation, the Coalition was in disarray over this vital issue and could not act. I took heart from two sayings: if you are hitting your head against a brick wall and its hurts, stop! And – my guiding principle – think global, act local.

Action on climate change was a priority for my supporters, for me and, I believe, the world, and doing nothing was not an option. Shortly after my election some of the Indi expats and their local friends approached me about their plan for the small community of Yackandandah – they had formed an organisation, Totally Renewable Yackandandah, with the goal of powering the town with 100 per cent renewable energy by 2022 and asked for support. Their energy and motivation were inspiring and I was determined to give them all help possible. I asked if we could take the idea and duplicate it across the electorate. Together, we formed a network and eventually a reference group, Totally Renewable Indi (TRI), based on the successful Indi Telecommunications Action Group, and had our first meeting in my office in 2016. There was broad representation across the electorate from local environmental groups, solar businesses and industry, the Victorian Government, local council representation from the Greenhouse Alliance, and ARENA sent a representative, as did Ausnet Services, the company that owned the electricity distribution network in most of Indi.

It was an active group that met every three months, sharing information, ideas and projects, including supporting applications for funding. In my regular meetings with Malcolm Turnbull I made sure that reports from TRI were an agenda item. At this stage he was progressing his first big foray into energy policy, the pumped hydro project Snowy 2.0. When we talked about TRI, he would open up his tablet, bring up Google Earth and we'd look at the topography of northeastern Victoria and discuss opportunities for pumped hydro. I would point out where I lived, west of the Kiewa Valley, which hosted mainland Australia's second-biggest hydro-electric scheme. I explained that my house and farm were fully solar-powered and off the grid, and that he and his wife Lucy were welcome to visit to view my setup. At the time, the Kiewa Valley and the region around Falls Creek were the largest producers of renewable energy in Victoria, through their generation of hydro power.

I found Turnbull open to new ideas and we shared an interest, a passion perhaps, for action on climate change. Eventually he directed his staff to set up appointments with the environment minister Josh Frydenberg, and while Malcolm didn't take up my invitation to visit Indi, Josh Frydenberg did.

We had moved a long way from the early days when ministers wouldn't come to Indi. With prime ministerial approval, more than 70 individuals from local businesses and industry met with the minister in communities across the electorate, and outlined what an empowered community could achieve and the opportunities to extend this model throughout rural and regional Australia, with isolated communities generating and managing their own electricity. I wanted Frydenberg to feel the energy and hear the community describe their actions and visions. It was a successful visit, leaving all the participants motivated and dedicated to being the change they wanted to see, with or without federal government support. I'm pleased to report that to this day Totally Renewable Yackandandah and Totally Renewable Indi continue to go from strength to strength with the support of Indigo

Power, our regionally based community-owned energy company. The point of the visit was to demonstrate that, if governments cannot make meaningful change, committed communities can and will.

While this action in the community was progressing, back in parliament I hadn't given up on trying to influence public policy on climate and energy and had introduced a private members bill capturing the idea of a distributed energy system co-existing with the centralised distribution system, based around large numbers of smaller, community-owned and operated power systems. Totally Renewable Yackandandah was the model: solar panels generating energy, large-scale battery storage and, where appropriate, pumped hydro, mini-grids with clusters of households sharing energy, and the beautifully named UBI, a mini computer developed by Ausnet Services to manage the administration and transactions. Sadly, there was no interest within the government, but there was within ARENA and with its support the first commercial mini-grid opened in Indi. In 2019, Mondo, a subsidiary of Ausnet, won two national awards from the Clean Energy Council for its innovations in Yackandandah.

Perhaps inevitably, given the Coalition's ideological gridlock, it was climate change and energy policy that led to the end of Malcolm Turnbull's prime ministership in August 2018. I found his downfall distressing. Not only had I developed a strong professional relationship with him as prime minister, but we shared perspectives on many topics, including action for climate, an Integrity Commission and the opportunity for a nationally coordinated approach to regional development. The overthrow of Malcolm Turnbull was for me one of the most personally distressing times in parliament. As the meetings and the scheming around his leadership took place, all I felt was a sense of doom for our country that has not left me. If what I was experiencing was the best the Coalition government could offer, what hope did we have? Differences about policy and leadership styles are part and parcel of all organisations and there isn't a group in the country that hasn't at some stage had to deal with this type of disruption. But, as a result, we learn problem-solving skills and dispute resolution strategies, going hard on the problem and soft on the person. As I watched the chaos unfold within the Liberal Party, I wondered, 'These are our leaders, where had these people been, and what had they done in their lives that they had not learnt these skills?'

In the week leading up to Malcolm's fall, as the Liberals broke off into groups and held their meetings and ballots, I was mindful that the government's numbers in the House were very close and he had said he would leave parliament if he was no longer PM. But I was fed up with the behaviour. I stressed to supporters of Dutton and Malcolm's eventual successor, Scott Morrison, that my commitment to work with the government had been given to Malcolm, not the Liberal Party, and they should not be under the impression that I was in any way sympathetic to what they were doing.

Under Morrison, there was a reshuffle of portfolios, which meant I needed to establish relationships with a whole new team of ministers and staff. The political agenda also changed with Morrison's new priorities, with which our office needed to become acquainted. The impact of the drought was on his list, as was the National Disability Insurance Scheme and protecting Australia's triple-A credit rating, and I recall religious freedom getting the odd mention. The workload was heavy and frenetic.

I found Morrison approachable and genuinely interested in building a positive relationship. He was also transactional and ready to cut a deal, which, given my commitment to my electorate of 'no deals', was problematic. Certainly, he knew that with Malcolm Turnbull leaving parliament, he would need either me, Rebekha Sharkie or Bob Katter on side and, as it happened, it was Bob who made that deal. At my first meeting with Morrison, he told me he understood Malcolm and I had a productive working relationship and he wanted something similar. He appointed a staff member to be the liaison with my office and arranged fortnightly meetings where we reviewed legislation and voting intentions.

Our relationship came under great strain during the Medevac debate in early 2019. This legislation was controversial as it offered seriously ill refugees in offshore detention a pathway to be transferred to Australia for urgent medical treatment. He was not pleased when I voted with the opposition and the government lost the vote on the floor of the House, which meant the passage of the legislation. I do not regret voting for Medevac, and I knew that I had the backing of my electorate on this legislation. I believed then, as I do today, that Australia's policy towards asylum seekers is unconscionable. We can do better, and be better, on this issue.

There was something close to a completion of the circle of my parliamentary life not long before it came to an end. In late 2018, with Australia in the grip of yet another terrible drought and rural Australians desperately in need of support and a new way forward when it came to dealing with our water problems, the agriculture minister David Littleproud introduced the Future Drought Fund Bill. As soon as I read it, I concluded that this legislation was falling way short of its potential. I was confident that on this subject and this legislation I could add value. I knew how important it was to engage with communities around drought and noted there was no evidence of community engagement in the preparation of the legislation. This problematic legislation came at a good time for me. The government had slipped into a minority position; along with the other crossbenchers, I held the balance of power. And I had established lines of communication with the agriculture minister and the prime minister. At that stage, I had confidence that I could have a serious effect on this issue and this government policy.

When Scott Morrison became prime minister, he appointed the former National Party leader Barnaby Joyce as his drought envoy. A summit followed soon after and the Future Drought Fund Bill was the result. The fund was to be paid for out of the Building Australia Fund, which had laid dormant since the 2014–15 financial year. It contained a sizeable pot of money. Joyce had introduced the policy but he was now a backbencher, so it was Littleproud's job to manage the legislation. The legislation looked to me to be ineffectual and shallow, and Littleproud had little ownership of it, which was fortunate for me. I had a positive working relationship with him. At my invitation, he had visited Indi earlier in the year and been a guest speaker at the Northeast Agricultural dinner. He also shared my interest in funding for rural local governments and the future of regional Australia.

But this episode was of a piece with my progressive sense of disappointment in the National Party during my time in the parliament. Clearly, quite a few National Party stalwarts were good enough to give me enormously valuable guidance along the way. However, all too often for my liking, the party's MPs at the federal level either took the easiest route or did not do their due diligence with policy areas that were vital to their constituents.

In a similar way as I had with Malcolm Turnbull when he was PM, during my regular meetings with Scott Morrison, where we would go through proposed legislation, including the drought bill, I made it plain to him that I didn't think much of it. He said he expected me to support it because it was 'about building pipes and building water infrastructure to make Australia resilient for drought'. When I heard him talking this way, I concluded that he'd swallowed a line put out by the irrigation lobby. I couldn't really believe that he thought the answer to the drought was to spend $100 million a year on pipes and dams and I resolved to make sure that did not happen.

Soon after, at the Speaker's Christmas drinks, an annual event bringing together most members of parliament and from my perspective an opportune time for some serious networking, I asked a senior regional Cabinet minister about the background of the legislation. He gave me the same line the prime minster had given me: 'Cathy, you'll really support that. It's about all these pipes and making sure we've got infrastructure when the drought comes'. I assumed these had been the words used in the presentation given to Cabinet. They were all spouting this simplistic idea, and I realised they didn't get the real potential of this funding nor appreciate that effective management and preparedness for drought was also about people and their attitudes, not only infrastructure.

As soon as this dawned on me, I sought a meeting with David Littleproud. I made sure not to go on my own and fortunately my fellow independent, Kerryn Phelps, who had only a few months earlier won Malcolm Turnbull's former seat of Wentworth, also wanted to meet with him and we both took staff. I must have gone in pretty hard during the meeting, because Kerryn told me afterwards that she'd never seen such effective lobbying. I explained that I was not usually that forceful. But the fact was, I was passionate about this and I could not stand to see such bad policy that would affect communities like mine and not significantly help them with managing future drought. With

IS THIS THE BEST OUR POLITICS CAN BE?

my background as a consultant to many of the agricultural research and development corporations, and with my time in leadership roles with Women in Agriculture, I was very familiar with impacts of drought, the various viewpoints on how industry wanted it managed and the long list of failed policy. I'd been working in this area for 15 years and, as well as the knowledge, I still had strong networks across most of the agricultural industries. I hit the phones.

My assumptions that this bill would fail were supported and, while the overall allocation of funding was welcomed, the details of how it would be allocated left a lot to be desired.

My team and I started putting together amendments to improve the bill and get it away from the simplistic pipes-and-dams framework. This was going to be a good one to win; when you have the balance of power, and there's no strong ownership of legislation, and you are across all the details, no-one really wants to argue with you. Though one politician did argue with me in a manner of speaking: Labor's infrastructure spokesperson, Anthony Albanese. He had earmarked the billions of dollars sitting there in the Building Australia Fund for Labor's spending programs on the other side of the upcoming 2019 election, which Labor was expecting to win. Barnaby Joyce knew about the fund. He has made some bad calls in his time but he is a politically smart operator and he had outsmarted the Labor team by tying the money from that fund to the drought fund. Albanese and his agriculture spokesperson Joel Fitzgibbon kept accusing me playfully of taking their money. My view was that the money was there to be spent and better that it be used properly.

In any event, Labor worked with me as I developed my amendments and its MPs voted for them, ensuring they got through. My amendments were primarily around improving governance and consultation.

They made the bill transparent by requiring a four-year plan based on consultation with the industry, regular reports to parliament and handing responsibility for ensuring environmental, social and economic outcomes were reached to the Productivity Commission. The government and all crossbenchers voted for the amended bill, which meant my amendments were accepted and eventually became the law.

The final passage of the drought bill happened towards the end of February 2019, as my time as the member for Indi was about to wind up. There were two satisfying aspects of this. Politically, it was going to make it easier at the upcoming election for Voices for Indi to push back at the stock criticism against all independents that they cannot do or achieve anything. In fact, every time the Nationals or the Liberals ran that line, Helen Haines simply replied, 'Drought bill'. It was so effective early in the campaign that they stopped running it after a while. There was now so much evidence of what we'd been able to deliver. Having the balance of power helped in this instance – of course it did. But, and this was the other satisfying element for me, the way we handled this issue demonstrated how much value we, and the crossbench generally, added to the making of policy and the lives of the people who had put us there as their representatives.

This was one of the high points in my time as the member for Indi. I was an Australian woman in agriculture who knew a bit more on this vital subject than the men who thought they had all the answers, and I managed to make a real difference for the better. In terms of impact, this was the piece of legislation that I was involved in shaping that had the greatest ongoing benefit for rural Australians, including farming businesses in my electorate. The fund will provide $100 million a year in perpetuity.

Chapter 13

A SURVIVAL GUIDE

On 4 April 2019, I gave my final speech in the House of Representatives with few hints of the nervousness that had informed some of my first appearances in the chamber. Many members of my family were there in the public gallery, including some of the Indi expats who had come up with the idea that I should become the member for Indi – something that had seemed quite fanciful to me at the time. The veteran press gallery photographer Mike Bowers took some wonderful pictures on that day. They captured my chief emotions: my joy and relief that I'd made it through. Back in 2013, I had taken a huge leap. Making a safe seat marginal was only part of what I was aiming for; I'd wanted to make sure that by the time I left, my relationships would be intact and my community would be more engaged in politics. And I wanted to have the respect of people who'd been my mentors through that process. Tony Windsor was one, and he was there that day. He had been one of my inspirations at the beginning. The fact that he travelled to Canberra for that final speech made this a powerful moment for me.

As I looked around the gallery and saw the faces of the original 12 who had formed Voices for Indi, the hub coordinators, the Indi Makers, so many young faces among the hundreds of volunteers and supporters who had made this people's movement possible, my gratitude was profound. We had done what we had set out to do – and along the way we established a strong process and had delivered significant policy achievements.

Our way of doing things required relentless effort. It had been difficult. There were no days off, no moments of dropping our guard. We had an objective of creating a community-wide political movement, with an effective community worker as the local member and had to learn how to get there as we went along, developing the process day by day. Mike Bowers' photos showed how being Indi's representative in Canberra had changed me. At the end, I looked more polished, stylish. I'd learnt how to dress to impress, how to be a public person. When I set out as a candidate, I had the basics and I had known a bit about community engagement, but I certainly didn't know how to build a mass movement; that had to be learnt. Nor had I been very good at working with large teams. Until then, I'd been a self-contained individual, extroverted at times but also quite private, pushing my way through the world. After taking that Saturday night phone call from Ben and Leah in 2012, I had to learn how to be part of a team where ideas and strategies and principles were subject to rigorous argument. Becoming an MP required taking on, to some degree, a public persona but it was still essential to stay true to who I was when I started. I couldn't let myself down, because letting myself down would mean letting the community down. I had wanted this to work but more importantly many thousands of women and men in Indi wanted it to work.

When I was re-elected in 2016, together with senior staff and key supporters we agreed that now was the time to be bold. Being bold did not mean being hard, it was more about ensuring that we should push ourselves to get things done, deepen our connections with the community and bring along more young people and Aboriginal people.

We wanted the community to be proud that it had backed us, to feel justified in keeping me as its member because I had delivered what I said I would deliver.

And we wanted to ensure that our project lasted beyond my stint in parliament. I was feeling optimistic on that score. While I was being bold during my second term, I was also preparing to leave and was on the lookout for someone to step up to be the candidate. In January 2019, Voices for Indi, using a consultative, community-based process, appointed Helen Haines as the candidate they would support in the next election. When I made my final speech, I was 70 per cent sure that Helen would succeed me in the seat; the feeling I was getting back from the community was strongly in her favour.

One of the most important goals of a community-based movement should be to become self-sustaining, to go beyond its initial burst of enthusiasm and the original personalities who brought it together. If it doesn't get that right, there's a danger that the good work, the early achievements, can fall away. This is not, strictly speaking, a succession plan, although in some respects it resembles that. It's about holding together and preserving the values and aspirations that form the basis of the movement. I was never the embodiment of Voices for Indi – I was merely its most visible public representative. That's how it worked, and it was one reason why it was not a wrench for me personally to step down.

I'd flagged my intention to leave to my Voices for Indi colleagues a while back and there had been some ongoing tension between me and a number of our people – don't ever think it's always sweetness and light in any organisation – over getting a selection process going. Once it was sorted out, in January at a Voices for Indi community-sponsored meeting in Benalla, 200 people selected Helen, who was one of three candidates. I knew Helen would be great. When I was having a tough day during our first campaign in 2013, I saw she had a special quality. I was with the campaign team, trying to film some TV ads in which I would speak to camera. Helen's husband Phil was the campaign manager and we were using their house on the outskirts of Wangaratta as the location. I was nervous because I was coming to the script cold. I hadn't been able to rehearse it and I was finding it hard to memorise. This was all new to me, and it started to become quite a chaotic experience. I was getting frustrated, finding the script too complicated.

Helen, who was doing her PhD in medical science at that time, took me inside her kitchen, gave me a cup of coffee, and started to workshop the words with me. Cam Klose, our wonderful media guy, had given up on me and tactfully headed off for a breather. This might not have been my finest moment as a candidate. Helen and I got the words together, going back and forth about what was working, and she was such a gift to me. Not only was she calm and sensible, she was good with words. I went back before the camera, we reshot and this time it worked out. I recall thinking that Phil was an innately political beast and very good at what he did, but his wife was going to be a really useful friend because she had a great feel for the community politics and she got the language. She had political nous.

When I started thinking about who may be interested in stepping up, I thought of Helen, I thought she had what it takes. I courted other women as well in that time. I tried to convince Judy Brewer to stand, which would have attracted a lot of attention, but Tim was sick with the cancer that would sadly take his life, and it wasn't possible. I was grateful that Helen agreed to put her hand up. And as you know from the beginning of this book, she definitely had the goods because on 18

May 2019 she created history by winning Indi – the first independent to follow another independent – while I was just a spectator.

When it was announced that I would not be recontesting and Helen would be our orange independent candidate, I saw the community transfer its loyalty to a bigger ideal. Truly they had supported me and now their loyalty was to the ideal that underpinned our movement. What we were all about was electing a strong independent person who could go on our behalf to Canberra. The fact that people understood this was enormously satisfying.

Was I surprised by the result of the general election, with the Morrison government getting across the line with a two-seat lower house majority? I wasn't paying much attention; my focus was on Indi. I don't cheer for either side. Like just about everyone, I thought the swing would go to Labor, as the opinion polls had suggested. But in our own electorate, I did experience a little of what the Labor Party campaign insiders must have been experiencing during the final days and weeks before election day. My early confidence about Helen's chances started to fade a little as I saw how much money the government was throwing at Indi, which we now know was part of the 'sports rorts' affair. Fortunately, the random spending promises didn't work as the government hoped in Indi. But there were still some disturbing wider outcomes in that election campaign that go to exactly what our community movement is all about: money can still buy political power.

When things settled down after the election, I saw more clearly what had happened: Clive Palmer's $90 million advertising campaign, designed to stop Bill Shorten becoming prime minister and shore up the government, had the biggest influence on the national result. Our position has always been that the parties are the parties, they do what they do for better or worse, and we will work with whoever wins office, but the impact of that money and that advertising, and the viciousness of the campaigning, made me feel sad for Australia, for our democracy. I also felt disappointed by what was done to Rob Oakeshott, who tried and failed to regain Cowper. He was subject to character assassination, especially by the National Party. It was ugly. This cannot be the way we conduct our politics. If independents are going to run and win, they should study the Cowper campaign because there's every chance that's the sort of warfare they'll find themselves engaged in.

I believe that only by standing up and arguing for something better will we improve our democracy and make politics more relevant. Relying on the traditional, two-sided political model will not generate enough change and will continue to leave large sections of Australian society feeling left out. This is especially so in rural and regional Australia. My arguments are not personal. But it seems clear to me that many electorates outside the big cities are being let down by their representatives. After spending six years in parliament, hand on heart, I do not know what the National Party stands for. For the most part, it's just there. It seems to me that too many of its federal MPs are tag-alongs, back-seat occupiers. The biggest policy proposal they talk about is a $9 billion inland freight route from Brisbane to Melbourne. Of course that is important, but for who? It's an uncontroversial piece of infrastructure and nothing special. Water policy is a fiasco. The National Party is nowhere intelligent on the Murray–Darling Basin, so in New South Wales the Shooters and Fishers Party gets all the running on that issue because at least it has a position. The party has its leadership tussles and its members hold their seats because they distribute money, with schemes like the sports rorts. That's what it seems to be about.

Unquestionably, they've had decent individuals in their system – people of integrity. Darren Chester, the member for Gippsland, is a strong advocate and well respected locally. There have been others – obviously Tim Fischer, but also Warren Truss. Solid men.

How many grassroots members would the National Party have in northeast Victoria? Very few, and they would be mostly older men who work really hard at election time putting up huge numbers of corflutes all around the place. But despite the fact there is a National Party state member based in Wangaratta – Tim McCurdy, who was good enough to give me advice when I was first elected – there is no genuine, ongoing connection between the party and communities, and little visibility, certainly in my part of the state. Ideally, I would have liked that not to be the case. If the National Party did what it should always have been doing, there would be no need for Voices for Indi.

The Coalition arrangements end up excluding too many sections of our society, especially in the bush. When the Fair Work Commission announced penalty rate cuts for hospitality and retail workers in 2017, the Labor Party tried to get the parliament to legislate to block the cuts. My attitude was that what Labor was proposing was an intervention in the system, which I thought was bad governance. The setting of penalty rates had been moved out of the jurisdiction of the parliament, away from politics, and it was rightly the responsibility of the independent commission. Now Labor wanted to bring it back into parliament for a vote. I couldn't support that. I knew I was likely to get some blowback from some workers in my seat, because penalty rates were such a touchy issue. To be coming out and saying 'Yes I'm going to vote for you to lose your penalty rates' meant I was in for a rough ride. Wanting to find out how other regional MPs were dealing with it, I approached a couple of my colleagues in the Nationals, and asked who in their party had coverage of industrial relations. The answer was no-one, because that portfolio had been allocated to a Liberal. This was my experience with the tertiary education bill in my first term being replayed. Did anyone keep a watching brief in the National Party given that the cuts could have different impacts in the regions compared with the cities? Again, no.

The determining factor was whether there was a portfolio; once the portfolios are handed out, that decides what policies the entire party will pay attention to. It's crazy. It dawned on me that for the whole of Australia, if a portfolio was held by a Liberal, Rebekha Sharkie and I were the only members of the House of Representatives actually looking at the regional implications of these policies. It was deeply disappointing to see this being played out.

I put it to the test with all the work I did on childcare when the minister for education Simon Birmingham was introducing changes to childcare funding and it was having an incredibly negative impact on the regions. I could not get a single National Party person to pick up my amendments, to talk about it or to take any interest in the impact on childcare. They wouldn't do it. I introduced a private members bill and I moved amendments to the legislation on childcare, and I recall experiencing an incredible level of frustration. In my speech and in a press release, I named all the National Party MPs sitting opposite who'd voted for the changes. One of the senior Nationals chastised me, telling me this wasn't the done thing, but I didn't agree. They needed to be called out for letting down their communities. Breaking that open is important, because the language that the party uses is 'We care for the country – we'll look after you if you vote for us', but I believe I showed that when an independent holds a seat that is marginal and competitive, the community's wishes will be more effectively represented.

The experience since 2013 in Indi is that voters will see through the conventional parties – and here I'm talking about the Liberals and the Nationals – if they are offered a better, more open, more trustworthy alternative. The sports-rorts scandal shone a light on a cynical and incoherent form of politicking. It was based on a raw calculation: the parties had a political need to hold or win a seat, so they just shot money in the direction of random parts of seats in the hope of picking up votes, without a plan for what they wanted to happen socially in those places. The National Party especially favours this practice. During the early part of 2019 and before the election, I grew tired of Bridget McKenzie as the sports minister visiting Indi to make a funding announcement where she would text me 10 minutes after the announcement, or 10 minutes before, in some distant town that I wouldn't be able to reach in time. A lot of local people were not happy. They wanted to know where their local member was when these announcements took place. So too did the local media.

The Liberal Party indulged in this behaviour as well. Its candidate at the 2019 election, Steven Martin, visited 50 towns in 50 days and then had funding announcements for each of those towns when I knew in some instances no formal application had been lodged. When he invited Victorian Senator Jane Hume to the electorate to announce $200,000 for a new scout hall in Myrtleford, I asked the mayor if he had known anything about this in advance. 'No, we only heard about it today', was his reply. I challenged Steve and wanted to know what his process was. I told him every single scout hall in every single town needed an upgrade like that, and that if he got elected I would campaign publicly until every single scout hall got their $200,000.

Everywhere I'd go, the constituents were complaining about it. I spoke to Mark Dreyfus, the shadow attorney-general, and he told me it shouldn't be happening. We both ended up writing to the Commonwealth auditor-general, who investigated the program and produced a damning report. Fortunately for Steven Martin, Helen won, so he didn't have to deal with me pursuing him around Indi asking where all the new scout halls were. And that was a lesson from this: the people of Indi couldn't be bought. They chose a straight-shooting community independent, despite the enticements.

I hope I've demonstrated with these stories that I'm passionate, not vindictive. When I was younger, I did believe that a person was their politics, which related to their social attitudes more than anything else. I had low tolerance for different perspectives and could be, if not rude, then off-hand. But as I started to take leadership roles in agricultural organisations, I wondered how I was ever going to get anything done if I went around cutting people dead. I had to learn how to go soft on the person and hard on the issue. I suppose I'd had a lighter version of this experience with my father who I loved dearly, but gee, he could be of his type at times. We butted heads pretty seriously about my desire to run my own farm, which he didn't think should be my kind of work. And our politics were different. I was more fluid: economically conservative and socially liberal. He taught me so much and we had a good relationship and I didn't want to let our disagreements get in the way.

Agriculture is predominantly a patriarchal system and I wanted to make it better for women, and that means the powerful men are eventually going to lose some power, and I suspect they know that. In bodies like the Victorian Farmers Federation, if I wanted to implement change, I had to learn how to manage up. That's why an independent has to come into politics with the intention of developing relationships that are above and beyond party politics. Despite what I've written about my annoyance with Bridget McKenzie, I have a great deal of personal respect for her as a woman surviving in the National Party. I think she was done over like a dinner by the Coalition system, losing her ministry over the sports-rorts affair when she was not the one who was ultimately in charge of it. She was a victim. She moved to Wodonga ahead of the 2019 election as a way of sounding out if she should run for the seat – she decided not to – and if I see her in the street I'll enjoy talking to her. I have no animosity towards her at all. I could see the politics of what she was doing, even if I didn't like it.

So just how did I survive in parliament? Certainly, it wasn't that people were always nice to me. I was not naïve, nor was I deaf. For example, if I got any sense that a male MP was being rude to me – and it happened a couple of times in my early years with a bit of sarcasm from the government side suggesting that I was just a waste of space – I wouldn't take it. Very early in the piece I set up a relationship with the whips on both sides, chiefly on the advice of Christopher Pyne, to talk with them because they organised everything. It wasn't beyond me to let the whips know in a gentle way over a cup of coffee that one of their team had made a sexist comment in passing. Could they possibly keep an eye out because I just needed their help with this and I didn't want it to become a whole public thing or be in conflict with one of their team, so if they could please very gently let this person know that it wasn't on, that would be great. I wasn't beyond defending myself by using the system to get things done. Scott Buchholz was the government whip at the time and was very open to doing anything he could to make sure that I was treated well. When you're operating on your own, you always need to know how to protect your space.

I don't believe that an independent can be a policy chameleon. If you stand for public office, you must have beliefs about the best direction for your society. I favour less government intervention in most circumstances. I believe in free trade and markets doing what they can do with a minimal amount of regulation. But policies such as these cannot sit outside a strong ethical framework. In fact, they cannot succeed without one. We must have people of morality in a government. We should be able to assume that our government will always work with the best of intentions for the community that it represents. Malcolm Fraser, who was prime minister when I worked for Mr Cameron, had that sort of morality. The other Malcolm, Turnbull, might have had it. I wanted to believe he did.

Politicians like to play around with the concept of ideology. Sometimes it's good, sometimes it's bad. When the COVID-19 pandemic was declared, the vogue in the Morrison government was to declare that this was not the time to be ideological. This then gave the government permission to run up large deficits that it would otherwise never tolerate. But why is it always okay to be so ideological about climate change? Is that not an emergency too?

The only explanation I can find for this disconnect is the power of the fossil-fuel lobbyists. If I'm right, this is sickening because the policy – or the wilful inertia that drives the government's overall approach – is not about good policy in the best interests of Australians, it's about who pays. What does it mean for people in the country? Farmers, businesses and families who rely on a healthy environment deserve something better. As I watched that 2019 election campaign and saw Clive Palmer's pages of ads in *The Age* every day, I thought this was not the Clive Palmer I know, at least on climate change, which I think he regards as real. The ads were not about getting his

Palmer United Party candidates elected, and none were, by the way; they were designed to bring down Bill Shorten.

That is Australia's reality. It's not only about money, it's about ideology and powerful people doing what they can with our political system in a really blatant way, and unless we change that, many, many communities in country Australia will be denied their rightful share of political power. As Tony Windsor says, 'One-third of the votes in Australia are held in the regions and the National Party currently holds the balance of power; never forget it. They just don't use it in a way that works.' We need to change how we use politics, how we make it work for us. If we want good governance and we don't want elections that can be bought and sold, we as a community have got to do the work.

In 2013 in Indi our strategy was for one in four voters to change their vote, and we could change the electorate. The formulation applies nationally too: if one in four regional voters changed their vote, that would be enough to change the country.

I was 30 when I finished working for Mr Cameron and went travelling around South America and set up a consultancy business to work with community groups to make the best use of government. I've now come full circle. I've finished the job of being a Member of Parliament. My next stage of life will be talking to people about what I've learnt: I want to encourage them to aim for what Voices for Indi achieved, which was not simply to disrupt conventional party politics once but to create sustainable change by electing successive independent candidates.

Chapter 14

YOU CAN DO IT

As I turn my mind to life after politics, I believe the task of helping Australia reach its potential through an engaged citizenry active in its democracy is critical and complex work. I believe independents and community politics hold a vital piece of the jigsaw. I hope my story inspires others to be part of this movement and are motivated to activate their courage muscle; to turn up, speak up and step up to leadership. In this final chapter, I offer some advice and a call to action, and share some reflections on my journey where both the pathway and the destination have truly shaped me.

Because I've championed the cause of the parliamentary independent from the beginning, I'm often asked how many independents should rightly sit in the House of Representatives. Do I have an ideal number? I don't. My starting point is good representation. I don't care what colour or shape our representatives are; I just want them to be professional. That is, professional in the way they go about representing the best interests of their constituents. I'm also asked if, having moved on from being the member for Indi, I'm going to create another movement or set up a party. Absolutely not. That's not my agenda. What I care about is having genuine competition in the system so that voters get the opportunity to make a choice among a range of quality candidates who can do the job.

I have no opinion about how people group themselves once they get into parliament. To me, their politics do not matter that much. If you've got quality people as parliamentarians and good leaders who can see beyond their own self-interest, they will be able to work together. Politics is a team effort, and without a quality team it will always be dysfunctional and produce lesser outcomes. My involvement as a political candidate and MP was predicated on demonstrating that competition is the way to improve how we're governed.

The reality in 2012 was that we had an adversarial system but we weren't using it. Indi had not been competitive for decades. The last time the Labor Party had won Indi was 1929 and it promptly lost the seat two years later. After that, various iterations of the Liberals and Nationals had held it. In 2013, we used the system and tried to make it work for us by pumping serious competition back into it. We succeeded. Indi is a contested seat. The Liberal and National parties view us differently now. Going down the independent path worked for us, but it might not work everywhere else. In other electorates, running strong Labor candidates with great community input in a safe Coalition seat might be the answer. Or the reverse: non-Labor candidates tapping into communities to win safe Labor seats that Labor has taken for granted. Personally, I have a bias for good women independent candidates who have had life experience, strong morals, know how to run an office and have decent knowledge about how to exist in the world outside politics. That's something I know a little about.

The Australian Election Study, which interviews a large sample of voters on each federal election day, has found a steady decline in voters' trust in government since the 2007 election. The problem of voter engagement is serious. We cannot have an effective democracy without engagement.

There are ways to tackle the problem. In Indi we saw our 110,000 voters as existing across a spectrum of political engagement. At one end were the people who disliked politics and would never want to think about it. At the other end were those who were devoted to the political contest. Most people were in the middle. They just want to live their lives, and for them the goings-on of politics are neither a preoccupation nor something to be avoided. My staff and I took a deliberate approach to win over this group. We didn't necessarily want to recruit them to our cause or get their votes. But we did view every constituent who came through the door as someone we could possibly engage in politics. We focused on constituent service in our office. We wanted to give everyone who contacted or visited a positive and satisfactory experience.

One of my staff had been a Qantas flight attendant, and we developed a model akin to flying with an airline. We weren't offering first class but we were going to give everyone a good experience in economy. When you fly, you're satisfied as long as you're treated respectfully by the cabin crew and you reach your destination in a timely manner. That's what we aimed for. Sometimes the staff wanted to devote days and days of their time to a constituent but that wasn't practical. Instead, we had to be content with delivering a professional experience, based on the understanding that we were there to serve our constituents.

In my final full calendar year as the member for Indi, in 2018, out of 110,000 constituents 32,415 individual pieces of correspondence came into the office and we opened 15,285 new cases. The numbers were similar the year before. I seriously doubt those sorts of numbers would be replicated in a safe seat held by a major party, because in safe seats many people lose the sense that their MP is there to help them. When a seat is locked up, with no chance of changing hands, the act of casting a vote is often just a formality for many electors.

Our approach created a significant workload in the office. Sometimes, if one of the staff were not up on the customer service, there would have to be a difficult conversation: 'Perhaps this job's not for you, because you actually need to care for people. That's what we're here for.' We could not afford to relax on this because it was one of the things that distinguished us from our major-party predecessor. Our level and type of constituent service was a point of difference.

Rather than concentrate on labels or how many independents we should have, instead ask this: how many professionally qualified politicians who understand constituent service, policy development, how parliament works, how the media works, can self-reflect and have a bit of humility, are there in the system? Not a lot.

The big picture in politics is all very well but what I know from my time as an MP is that, as an independent, I maintained a sharp focus on my electorate and tried not to allow the larger political debates and big-party controversies that constantly occupy the media's attention to inhabit my mental space or direct my behaviour. This was a key to our success, which may seem counterintuitive to some. First, we built much higher levels of voter engagement by getting things done at a constituent level, which challenged the predictable line that a vote for an independent was a wasted vote. My message to the electorate was 'I want to represent you and I will always do that. I will always put Indi first.'

By doing that and not trying to make myself a major national talking-head on every subject going, I managed to get some good things done in Canberra. I was regularly surprised by how people in Canberra treated me. I knew I had a vote they needed but it was more than that, it was also because I stuck to my knitting and everybody knew I was sticking to my knitting; I wasn't going to interfere and get involved with party politics. Both sides had a pretty clear idea of my agenda. I did not needlessly play the power card. I understood from my leadership experience pre-politics that your power was something you managed, not brandished about. I did play on the national political stage when I needed to: on drought policy, for example. I knew about that subject. I had credibility on it.

As an MP, I had an abiding interest in strengthening higher education facilities and opportunities outside the metropolitan cities. After my early experience thwarting the government's attempt to reduce the sector in rural and regional Australia, I continued to keep an eye on what was happening with higher education, as it was obviously a space where the Coalition was looking to make savings. In March 2018, I introduced a private members bill, the Higher Education Support Amendment (National Regional Higher Education Strategy) Bill, calling on the government to establish a strategy for regional tertiary education based on a four-year review process, with a commissioner to oversee its implementation. In the reshuffle after Malcolm Turnbull's departure later that year, I found a willing ear when Dan Tehan was appointed education minister. With his rural background, he was supportive of a separate rural and regional strategy, was a commissioner, and recognised the need to address the gap between urban and rural completion rates. In his June 2020 higher education policy, he announced his intention to appoint a Regional, Rural and Remote Education Commissioner to be a champion for regional education. The commissioner will advocate for a coherent policy response and will oversee the implementation and monitoring of the government's strategy. The lesson here is that it pays to plant the seed if the opportunity is there.

Late in my second term, I found myself taking much of the load of advancing the idea of a national integrity commission to deal with corruption within federal bodies. I believe it's an absolute must for the nation, as did many of my fellow crossbenchers. In the fractious period when the government's parliamentary majority was getting shaky, five of us on the crossbench raised a Matter of Public Importance on the subject. Malcolm Turnbull had flagged he might do something about establishing the sort of body we were looking for but then he was gone, replaced by Scott Morrison. It fell to me and one of my senior staff members to progress the idea. Rebekha Sharkie's office had done a good deal of work but she couldn't shoulder it all. She handed over her material, prepared with Transparency International Australia, and my staff got to work.

My staff worked for three months, enormous hours with the parliamentary counsel and Transparency International Australia drafting a bill. We shared our draft around Parliament House and the respect for our office, and for my staff, who had considerable experience working at a high level for various departments, meant we were taken seriously. We were able to win Labor's support. (The government took it up too, but proceeded to hasten slowly afterwards.) That had a national impact, at least in part because our office was viewed as skilled, not afraid of hard work and capable of delivering. It's an object lesson for some of the more enthusiastic younger people I've known who love politics and want an independent to make a big impact on Canberra. I tell them that the competition with everyone trying to play on the big national stage is intense. If an independent starts at the local level and looks after their community, that will garner respect and lead eventually to the bigger national policy wins. Back home is where the joy of the job lies.

Community politics is not for the faint-hearted. One of the challenges of being an independent was how exposed you are; all the time you're in the public view and there's no place to hide. You are what you are – with your staff, with the community – and you are incredibly vulnerable if you haven't learnt how to look after yourself. You've actually got to be comfortable in your skin. If you're not, other people will inevitably try to pull the rug out from under you and you'll look for excuses. I could have done that many times, pleading that I didn't deserve to be attacked because I was just a woman or only a backbencher. But if you're safe in your own identity and you're secure in your own ability, and have the backing of your community, you can hear criticism for what it is, look at it and accept that your critic might have a point that you should take on board.

The longer I was in the job, the better I got at doing it. By the time I was getting close to finishing, I used to have interesting exchanges with my staff, who, like a lot of us, don't like listening to complaints. A constituent would make a complaint and I'd tell them to take down the details so I could call the person back. My view was that it didn't matter if the person was an habitual critic, I'd still call them. I'd listen to whatever it was that had made them disgruntled. I suspected that person was unlikely to like me or even vote for me but they'd been heard, and we could not afford to lose that basic respect that was central to the values of Voices for Indi. Trust is such a precious commodity in our politics, and it comes from respect. There's too little trust between the major parties. Tony Abbott never respected Julia Gillard, he laid into her in the most disrespectful way. Many people see that and think: 'I don't behave like that in my family, I don't behave like that in my business. If I behaved like that I'd be out of business.' It's such an unnecessary way to behave and it puts people off politics.

There are many people of good will, skills and relevant community and business experience who could make very good parliamentarians but they're turned off by what they see on the trust and respect score. I know from my Women in Agriculture networks that there is not a woman who runs an Australian agricultural business with her husband and her extended family who would not be capable of holding her own in parliament. These women are in multi-million-dollar businesses, managing staff, droughts, fires, floods, communities, trade and commercial issues and government regulations. I know they could rise to the occasion, but they rarely raise their hands to try to become parliamentarians.

The problem is, they feel shut out of contention, seeing politics as a game played by men – mostly men, but some women – who have made politics their vocation from an early age. When we ran the volunteer program in our Parliament House office, my favourite thing to show them was a list of the politicians by profession and past work experience. I would take them through the list. We would go through by party the qualifications and the occupations of the people who are in parliament and there were so many occupations not represented. Until Labor's Ged Kearney took the seat of Batman at a by-election in 2018, there was no qualified nurse sitting in the parliament, for example. There were no childcare workers, few teachers. The diversity is not there, the lived experience is not there. This is where the opportunity for independents beckons. When I was first elected, I was a single woman farmer and consultant who was a few months short of 60, with zero direct political experience. Would I have won a major party preselection?

There is definitely a great opportunity for women to step into this space. It's no coincidence that increasing numbers of women from outside the big parties have taken previously safe seats from the Liberals. Rebekah Sharkie has won Mayo three times, Zali Steggall defeated Tony Abbott in Warringah in 2019 and Kerryn Phelps won Wentworth in a 2018 by-election. We have all shown what can be done. But there are things that every independent candidate should be mindful of. Campaigns cost money. Get yourself set up properly to receive donations. The rules are made by the parties for the parties, and in 2013 an early task was sorting out administrative arrangements for accepting donations. We researched the Australian Electoral Commission rules and checked in with my accountant: To whom to write cheques? Was it the candidate? Was it Voices for Indi? Their view that although Voices for Indi was an incorporated body, I was the candidate, so I set up a separate bank account and we were rigorous in following the rules and ensuring that all the money donated to the Cathy McGowan Campaign was receipted. Which was fine until tax time came around and my accountant informed me that the $180,000 in donations would be considered by the Australian Tax Office as personal income, leaving me with a $15,000 tax bill, because I wasn't a party. A cautionary tale.

The party structure also has its advantages in terms of lightening an MPs workload. As an independent, I didn't have the luxury of relying on a party to create or test policy, which placed enormous demands on my staff. In 2016 Malcolm Turnbull allocated two extra staff and that made a big difference to my ability to run the office and manage the work load, particularly the oversight of the parliamentary legislative program. In my office I was blessed with loyal, skilled and capable staff who were prepared to buck in, learn on the job, help each other and undertake continuous professional development. However, the jobs are big, they are not particularly well paid and there are only a small number of people who can do the type of work a community-based independent wants done. There is no formal training, qualification or course available in Australia and the career path is mostly an on-the-job apprenticeship. Experienced political or parliamentary advisors are rarely found in the country, and are usually programmed to look at the world through a conventional party-political prism, which generally does not involve treating an MP's constituents as the most important audience at all times.

As an independent, it felt like I was always performing a balancing act. I'd have to make decisions, lots of them, all happening at the same time and, as often as not, I might not be across all the detail, and rarely are things what they seem to be on the surface, but you've got to make these big calls anyway. Part of the balancing act is to maintain your distance emotionally and trust your judgment; whatever you decide is the best decision at the time, based on the information you have. Stick with that and don't waste time beating yourself up about it.

And it pays to resist the impulse to be cynical. You campaign on offering something better from outside the traditional political paradigm. But you have to embrace the reality that if you put your hand up and seek to become a Member of Parliament you're looking to become part of the system – albeit a different and unusual part of it. What kept me going, and I believe that every independent needs to feel this way, was my faith and trust in the system. That system was flexible enough to enable Voices for Indi to take shape, then for us to carry our message throughout Indi and ultimately for me to be elected. As I said earlier in this book, the system was initially designed to accommodate that sort of grassroots, participatory democracy, it's just that our parties have found ways to get around it.

We have a good system and it can work. That's how I operate. I don't begin from a negative starting point. We definitely need to improve it by reframing it and we must work through an iterative process. Australia needs to work out once again how it does democracy more meaningfully. It won't happen all at once. I have faith and trust and hope that we will do that, because there are enough good people in our communities to make it work. I balance that with my absolute realism that the system also has a lot of bad practices that need to be wiped out. I don't pretend they're not there.

The essence of my political mission as an independent was to see our democracy for what it is and work on the things that were bad. I concluded that I couldn't make the big changes but I could work where I had some influence, and motivate people to be the change we wanted to see, to do that with hope and respect, with the anticipation that people will see best practice and want more of it. That was what guided me rather than trying to solve all the problems. I knew they were there. Things were what they were; I could work around them but I always kept thinking, 'Being the change you want to see is the most powerful thing I can do'.

In Indi, we showed what can be done. I have no doubt that there are many other parts of Australia where our experience can be replicated, but those who try it need to get their independent campaigns properly organised. No two electorates are the same, either in their make-up or in their political circumstances. The Voices for Indi setup is unique: our personalities, our geography, our history. But we learnt a lot that has to be of value to other communities and we want to share it. That's one of the key reasons I've written this book. We were able to do what we did because our local system was broken. I don't know how broken a system has to be in every circumstance, but we found the crack in Indi and we got organised and we went into the crack and we pushed it open. I believe it's incredibly difficult to run successfully as an independent if the system isn't broken in some way. The fact is, when there is a shared problem in your electorate, it enables the community to coalesce and change the status quo. This is the piece of political analysis worth doing in the first instance: is the system broken enough and can we make that crack big enough to push it open?

The next question to ask is: can you get organised? Raising community engagement up to a vibrant level is a massive challenge. You cannot afford for it to be shambolic or done in a scattergun way; it has to be coordinated and built upon steadily. Take the example of the Victorian seat of Mallee in northwestern Victoria at the 2019 election. The seat has belonged to the Country/National Party since its inception in 1949. In late 2018, the sitting National Party MP Andrew Broad, an assistant minister, announced he was leaving the seat after a personal controversy that found its way into the public domain. That was an example of the system being broken. An independent could have won Mallee at the election but they weren't able to organise the preference flows well enough – a great pity. Thirteen candidates stood at the election, three of them independents. I was busy with Helen's campaign in Indi, but I was watching this from the other side of the state. I rang a few of the candidates and suggested they get together and run a ticket, as I thought they were missing their chance to dislodge the Nationals. In my experience, one main candidate is needed, someone who is prepared to do all the follow-up work – the coordinated footslog to gather support and agreement on preferences. Without that, you cannot harness enough properly directed community support to establish a substantial local profile.

At the election, the National Party primary vote in Mallee fell from 64.3 at the 2016 election to 27.8 per cent. The Liberal candidate attracted 18.8 per cent. The independents together won 21.5 per cent of the vote. If a single independent had run and picked up most of that combined independent vote, he or she might have come in second on primaries and potentially been able to attract preferences from

Labor and minor party voters. At the very least, it was possible that the seat could have been moved into the marginal column. Instead, the preferences were distributed in the usual National–Labor split and the Nationals' candidate secured 66 per cent of the preferred vote, hardly any change at all from 2016. You just can't win against the parties if you're not as organised as them. The inability to be pragmatic about such things because you're full of idealism about changing the world can be a curse in politics.

A final comment: our experience in Indi is that if you're going to upend the political orthodoxy by turning a safe seat independent, you've got to find a way to get national media attention, even though you intend to run in the campaign and as an incumbent on community-driven issues. It only takes one spot. Tony Windsor urging Indi voters to back me over Sophie in 2013 during a television interview was mine. Helen had a similar experience in 2019. Twelve days out from election day, she appeared on the panel on the ABC show *Q&A*. Rebekha Sharkie had been invited but she couldn't come across to Melbourne, so the producers asked Helen, who performed very well and got a great response from the local people. The value of national media exposure is that it suggests you, as the candidate, can rise to a level of prominence that makes people in the community think you actually can do it in Canberra. Telling the community you can do it in Canberra doesn't work: it needs that level of external endorsement.

Winning the way we have done in Indi has not been about luck. Communities like Indi's that enter the political realm will rarely be able to compete on an even playing field or have the resources to campaign in the way the big parties can. But we have so many other strengths and capacities that can be turned to our competitive advantage. We need to reframe the political competition.

Being the member for Indi was not the making of me; it was the culmination of everything I had lived through and learnt and loved – the work I had done, the people I had met, my family, my community, the land. I am privileged to have had this unique opportunity. Being the member for Indi gave me a platform to talk about the issues that are important to me and our nation, an opportunity to practise my leadership skills in my community where I belonged and which I love and care about, and it enabled me to work with my extended family and support many young adults to act on issues of real interest and relevance to their future. By being the member for Indi, at a personal level I grew in courage and confidence, and I hope patience and tolerance, and I discovered skills I didn't know I had.

My call to action is to those who care about politics; if you're about service and social justice and making the world a better place and truly tackling some of the issues of our time, being a rural and regional independent with a community that backs you has to be one of the best jobs in the world. I'm happy to recommend it. And really, you will never know if you never have a go.

ACKNOWLEDGMENTS

There have been many thousands, even tens of thousands of people who have played significant parts in this story; to each and every one, a deep and sincere thank you. In acknowledging the gifts and generosity of everyone who stood up and spoke up, I make a deeply personal request: 'Please stay the distance, now is not the time to rest'.

I would like to put on record my thanks specifically to the people of Indi, whose trust, commitment and agreement to engage have created the axis for this movement and foundation for this story. And closely linked is the other community that enabled and facilitated the unfolding of this adventure and that is the community that constitutes our national parliament, those who work tirelessly and behind the scenes in the big white house on the hill.

Within the Indi community I acknowledge members of the central campaign committee and hub coordinators for the 2013 and 2016 elections and my staff over those six years.

Voices for Indi and orange campaigners including: Alana Johnson, Amanda Aldous, Angela Killingsworth, Anne Shaw, Ali Pockley, Ben McGowan, Cam Klose, Chris Hazel, David Godkin, Denis Ginnivan, Di Shepheard, Di Goonan, Glenis Rice, Helen Lemke, Jacqui Hawkins, Jan Avery, Jane Taylor, Jane Kearley, Jill Howard, John Davis, John Mahony, Julie de Hennin, Jude Scarfe, Judy Ryan, Karen Nankervis, Lauren Salathiel, Leah Ginnivan, Liz Wood, Margaret Brickhill, Mark Howard, Michelle Dunscombe, Nick Haines, Phil Haines, Roberta Baker, Roland Wahlquist, Ross Kearney, Rowan O'Hagan, Ruth McGowan, Sal Kimber, Susan Benedyka, Sylvia

Holloway, Tammy Atkins, Trish Curtis, Tony Lane, Tony Perrott and Tricia Hazelegger.

My staff: Barb Strand, Cam Klose, Catherine Morgan, Christine Thorpe, Di Thomas, Elise Wenden, Fiona Roberts, Georgina Curtis, Karen Anderson, Karen Keegan, Karen Nankervis, Kerryn Lee, Jacqui Hawkins, Jane Still, Jeremy Mickle, Jill Smith, Julie de Hennin, Leah Coles, Leah Ginnivan, Lou Armstrong, Marion Rak, Mark Earp, Michelle Cowan, Natasha Lobban, Nick Haines, Peter Kenyon, Rod Klein, Roberta Baker, Simon Crase, Steve Burke, Steve Cooper, Tas Vaughan, Tia Reid, Sara Gerardi, Scott Peebles and Sean O'Neill.

In the community that is the Australian Parliament, the members of the House of Representatives during the 44th and 45th parliament's crossbench deserve special mention: Adam Bandt, Andrew Wilkie, Clive Palmer, Julia Banks, Kerryn Phelps, Rebekha Sharkie and Bob Katter. In 2013 I was the first woman on the crossbench, and when I said goodbye there were four; across the differences of policies, electorates and life experience, we made a concerted effort to give voice to the more than one-quarter of Australians whose number one vote is not for the major parties. Together with your staff, I valued your company, advice, collegiality, professionalism and most of all your friendship. In due course I will look forward to reading your memoirs, reflections and analyses which I know will add great value to the nation's understanding of the role of the crossbench and its contribution to keeping the 'ship of state' afloat.

As an independent Member of Parliament, getting my voice heard via the mainstream media was an essential part of the job, so I thank the media and the press gallery, as well as the regional media in northeast Victoria, who from the early campaign days and always in parliament were interested in Indi and me as the representative. A particular

ACKNOWLEDGMENTS

acknowledgment to all at ABC television and national and regional radio who regularly gave me time and were interested in our issues, to Gabbie Chan and the team at *The Guardian*, Michelle Grattan and the team at *The Conversation* and University of Canberra, and Margo Kingston and the team at *No Fibs*, your work made a difference. And as it's not only about voice, to all the photographers who answered that call for an extra image, I am very grateful.

In legislating and ensuring evidence-based policy, many of the peak bodies assisted with research and advocacy. I acknowledge the work of the following in drafting private members bills and preparing speeches and amendments: the National Farmers' Federation President Fiona Simson, amending the drought legislation; Transparency International Australia's AJ Brown, drafting the legislation for an federal Integrity Commission Against Corruption and Code of Conduct for MPs; the Australian Council for Social Security's Cassandra Goldie, for general advice including the Social Security Commission; La Trobe University Vice-Chancellor John Dewar, head of campus at Wodonga Guin Threkeld, Charles Sturt University Vice-Chancellor Andy Vann, the Rural University Network and Universities Australia for various legislation on the university sector; Rural Australians for Refugees' Marie Selstrom, for various legislation, particularly Medivac; Anne Bowler of the National Association for Mobile Services for Rural and Remote Families and Children, for changes to childcare services; the Border Rail Action Group's Bill Traill and John Dunstan, for advocacy for funding for the northeast train line.

In the electorate so many answered my request to participate in the many Indi action and references groups, covering energy, telecommunication, transport, health, asylum seekers, community services, aged services, housing, water and agriculture. Thanks to Darren

Moffitt and Chris Thorn for linking me with many Aboriginal and Torres Strait Islander peoples; to the councillors and staff of Indi's local governments of Alpine, Benalla, Indigo, Mansfield, Moira, Murrindindi, Tawong, Wangaratta, Wodonga, and towards the end Strathbogie, I am grateful to you for making the endless trips to Canberra to lobby, advocate and turn up. Thanks also to the Albury Mayor and staff who together with Wodonga Council created the basis for the Albury Wodonga Regional Deal.

To the Indi 27, who were unjustly pursued, I am so very sorry you had to experience what happened; it wasn't fair, just or right, and the way you managed the affair showed your values and courage. I am tremendously proud of you and always grateful.

In bringing this book to fruition, so many worked their magic of taking an idea and bringing it to reality: Louise Adler and the team at Monash University Publishing for your persistence and creativity; Sir Andrew Grimwade for sparking the idea; Shaun Carney for being the book enabler, wrangler and facilitator; and Yael Cohn for translation of hours of audio.

To my family, siblings, niblings and partners, you were there at the beginning and at the end and kept the faith during the middle bits: Di, Frances, Helen, John, Liz, Mim, Paul, Tricia, Veronica, Ruth, Rebecca and your children and all the cousins and extensions. And David Wolfenden and Judy Brewer for your watchful and loving support and good advice.

It is not possible to adequately thank all the individuals and organisations who contributed to my election and work as an MP over the six years. My hope is that, through this book, you know your work is valued and appreciated, and with your support the 'Indi way' will continue to grow from strength to strength.

ABOUT THE AUTHOR

Cathy McGowan came to national attention when she won the seat of Indi as an independent in 2013, becoming the first female independent to sit on the crossbench. Winning the seat of Indi, after the Coalition had held the seat for 34 years, was a watershed moment. Indi became 'Exhibit A' for future political campaigns – from Kerryn Phelps as the Member for Wentworth to Zali Steggall in Warringah. The community backed McGowan again in 2016 for a second term, including during the minority government of Scott Morrison where, together with the crossbench, she held the balance of power. In 2019 she was thrilled to be part of the campaign that saw Dr Helen Haines elected as Indi's second female independent, a win that made Australian political history.

During her time as a politician Cathy actively worked in Parliament to develop policy around regional development, a national integrity commission, a code of conduct for politicians, as well as drought policy. In 2019 she was awarded The Accountability Round Table award for political integrity. She is an Officer of the Order of Australia, a Churchill fellow and lives very happily on her farm in the Indigo Valley in northeastern Victoria.

For more information about Cathy's time in parliament, details of speeches, legislation, pictures, and connections to Voices for Indi, please go to www.cathymcgowan.com.